MAKE
WINNING
A HABIT

MAKE
WINNING
A HABIT

RICK PAGE

McGraw-Hill

New York   Chicago   San Francisco
Lisbon   London   Madrid   Mexico City   Milan
New Delhi   San Juan   Seoul   Singapore
Sydney   Toronto

ISBN 0-07-146502-2

McGraw-Hill books are available at special quantity discounts to use as premiums and sales promotions, or for use in corporate training programs. For more information, please write to the Director of Special Sales, Professional Publishing, McGraw-Hill, Two Penn Plaza, New York, NY 10121-2298. Or contact your local bookstore.

This book is printed on recycled, acid-free paper containing a minimum of 50% recycled, de-inked fiber.

Library of Congress Cataloging-in-Publication Data
Page, Rick, 1947–
    Make winning a habit / by Rick Page.
        p. cm.
    Includes bibliographical references.
    ISBN 0-07-146502-2 (alk. paper)
    1. Sales management. 2. Selling. 3. Customer relations. 4. Sales personnel-Training of. I. Title.
    HF5438.4.P33 2006
    658.8—dc22   2006007363

To my wife, Pam

Love Lifted Me
Psalm 91
Proverbs 31
1 Corinthians 13
Philippians 4

CONTRIBUTORS AND EDITORS

Dr. Susan Adams, Bentley College

Doug Adams, President and CEO, SOLX, Inc.

Ken Allred, CEO, Primary Intelligence, Inc.

Ken Cornelius, President and CEO, Siemens One, Inc.

Frank DeSalvo, Research Director, Gartner, Inc.

Jan DeSalvo

Jim Dickie, Partner, CSO Insights

Joe Galvin, Group Vice President, Global Sales Field Operations, Gartner, Inc.

Rusty Gordon, CEO, Knowlagent

Rob Jeppsen, Senior Vice President, Commercial Loan Sales, Zions Bank

Jay Litton, Director of Sales, Central Region, Macrovision Corporation

Bruce McCalley, President, The McCalley Group

Jeff Mitchell, Executive Vice President, Americas, Manhattan Associates

Steve Garland, National Sales Manager, Epson America

Jim Ninivaggi, Director, Sales Performance Practice, SiriusDecisions

Ryan Parker, Account Manager, Manhattan Associates

Terry Turner, Senior Vice President, Sales and Marketing, Harcourt Assessment

Cal Wick, Founder and CEO, Fort Hill Company

ACKNOWLEDGMENTS

The talented principals and staff of The Complex Sale, Inc., are a blessing. Their intelligence, innovation, cooperation, and good attitude enable the unique ability of the company to continuously push the envelope of sales thinking and execution and to maintain a positive quality of life among a partnership of friends.

Principals of The Complex Sale, Inc.—Jack Barr, Blake Batley, Peter Bourke, Charles Buffington, Brad Childress (president), Jerry Ellis, Rob Goodwin, Brian Enright, Jon Hauck, Nick Holbrook, Phil Johnson, Liz McCune, Daryl Newman, Joe Southworth, David Stargel, and Joe Terry.

Staff—Susan Hauser, Karen Hipes, Susan Jones, Julie Kirchner, Joan Marenda (my executive assistant and handler), and Scotty Fletcher.

Special acknowledgment to Scotty Fletcher—Scotty Fletcher is a journalist with experience ranging from newspapers in Big Sky, Montana, and Augusta, Georgia, to business magazines in Atlanta. She and I have spent countless hours elbow to elbow in research, co-writing, and editing. Her skill, intelligence, humor, and discipline have made writing this book possible in the given time.

We teach that a plan untested is a plan for failure. I learned from my wife, Pam, an English teacher, that the hardest part of writing is editing. Thanks to Liz and Joan for proofing the copy. Thanks to the many friends and experienced sales executives and consultants, as well as all the principals of The Complex Sale, Inc., who contributed to or helped edit this work.

CONTENTS

INTRODUCTION

A recent study by a major consulting firm showed that a large percentage of CEOs think that their sales forces are underperforming. I think that they are right. Product superiority wins less than half the time. The difference is a sales force that can consistently leverage your advantages through the right people and the right issues in the right accounts.

This book gives you a way to assess yourself and your organization to see how you compare with your true potential and how you compare with the best practices of the rest of the sales world. What you get out of this book depends on what your particular pain is and how much change you want in your sales organization.

Doing the same things year after year and expecting different results has been used as one definition of insanity. And a system cannot change itself from within. It needs input and feedback from outside to adapt to change.

Sales techniques and technologies obviously will continue to evolve as they have for the last 30 years. The firms we mention are the ones we are aware of, and I am sure we have missed some worthy others.

And some of the companies that we mention in this book could well be out of business by the time it reaches print. But the practices that they enable will be continued by other firms or inside sales organizations because they provide improvement and advantage.

However, a common pain of many sales executives is adoption—how to make any training or technology stick. Awareness alone of best practices will not yield competitive advantage—only consistent discipline and execution will. This book will share with you the ways that other firms have made competitive advantage happen.

SECTION I

BIGGEST PROBLEMS, BEST PRACTICES

MANAGERS, TELL ME WHERE IT HURTS

How does a sales organization measure its true potential anyway? Making quota is an arbitrary measure; it just keeps your job in most places. But how much of the pie *could* you have gotten if you had performed to your full potential? What if each rep had made goal? What if all the reps had won *every* deal they pursued? Why don't they? What if discounts had been one percent less? What if new people got up to speed faster? What if they knew when to qualify out of bad deals? What if new products had been launched better? What if you had retained all your best reps? What is the gap between what you did do and what you *could* do?

And if there is a gap between what you *know* to do and *how* your organization is actually performing, then what is causing this weakness in execution, and how can you get better?

My first book, *Hope Is Not A Strategy*, generated more than 150 speeches and gave me the opportunity to evaluate hundreds of sales organizations worldwide. In meeting with these sales executives, three recurring themes surfaced: (1) common knowledge is not always common practice, (2) some sales executives are satisfied with merely catching up to the state of the art 15 years ago because it's what they are comfortable with, and (3) very few sales organizations are closed-loop continuously improving systems—instead, they improve in fits and starts.

There often seems to be a gap between what companies *know* to do and *how* they consistently perform. Although there are processes in place, many have fallen into disuse. Moreover, what sales managers really want to know is, how *do we* compare? What are the differences between what we're doing and the best practices of great sales organizations? How do we make anything stick? Finally, what innovations do we need to get ahead? And then how do we *stay* ahead?

This was all so natural when I was a sales rep. But now, I'm a manager and the challenges are all different. How do I get it out of *my* head and into *their* heads?

I just accepted a job managing a 100 person sales force that has consistently missed their forecast and quota quarter after quarter.

Though some of our people have good individual selling skills, they lack strategy. I'm not always sure they are in the right accounts or selling to the right people. There is no consistent process.

There's a CRM (client relationship management) tool in place, but no consistency of usage. Most salespeople use one tool for overall strategy, another for pain and linkage, and still another for account analysis—all from different vendors. Some don't use anything.

None of them are integrated and most of the time, forecasting is done on spreadsheets.

As a whole, our salespeople are short-term, opportunistic, revenue-focused, beginning every quarter thinking about the quarter at hand, rarely planning ahead. Most deals are ignored by the managers until they're in their last 90 days, sometimes less. Consequently, we lose and don't really know why.

We are a public company, so the ability to realistically forecast revenue is important. More than once, sloppy forecasting has forced managers to throw hugely discounted deals at customers before they're ready to buy. Last quarter, our CEO was embarrassed by a bad quarter caused by deal slippage and the stock dropped 20 percent. We can't let that happen again.

Some people do the right thing sometimes, but there is no consistency or discipline. There's no process or best practices in place for our most talented people to repeat their performance on a regular basis.

How do we make winning a habit around here?

HOW GOOD DO WE NEED TO BE? HOW GOOD IS GOOD?

Sales managers are unique among managers because they are almost always evaluated by *four* levels of performance:

1. Are you executing well enough what you *already know how to do*?

2. Are you at least executing the best practices of others in your industry?

3. What "next practices" and innovations can you do right now to get ahead of your competitors?

4. What feedback and continuous improvement processes will make these initiatives self-correcting organizational *habits* that drive perpetual advantage?

So what are the universal tools that *executives* apply to *sales managers*? That's easy—more pressure, flog the forecast, cheerlead, and maybe a little more money.

This is what *most* do, but not what the *best* do. They do it differently. To discover how they do it, you will need to take a little journey with me through this book. We will look at your practices, the practices many of our clients have used successfully, and the practices that are *executed well* by the very best in the business. And as we do it, we will explore a transformational map that can institutionalize those practices that you most need *right now*.

So let's get started. To begin, see if you can find yourself anywhere in the dozen most common problem areas that sales managers face.

THE DEADLY DOZEN: THE 12 BIGGEST PAINS SALES MANAGERS FEEL TODAY

When we talk to sales executives and managers at organizations and ask where they are weak, their responses generally fall into 12 categories.

1. Unclear Sales Process, No Common Language
"It takes forever to discuss an account around here. It takes almost an hour just to tell the 'story' and then I'm not sure if we've covered everything or have a clear strategy. We don't know what we don't know. There's got to be a more efficient and effective way to strategize deals on a global basis."

2. Missed Forecasts—Happy Ears, Surprises
"We understand that a positive mental attitude is good, but it can interfere with sound judgment. Some of our salespeople and managers are habitually overoptimistic about their chances of winning. How do we make sure that deals are being coached and evaluated by our more experienced managers?"

3. Qualification, Chasing Bad Deals
"We agree that there's a fine line between qualifying out and quitting. Everyone in sales knows that you don't get

into a deal you don't think you can win. But who decides what is winnable? We don't have agreed-upon criteria that constitute an unworthy deal."

4. Selling Too Low—We Can't Sell to Executives

"We have heeded the words of marketing and moved our offerings from 'products' to 'solutions,' requiring our salespeople to sell higher in the organization. The solutions have moved up to the strategic level, but many of our salespeople are still selling products and transactions too low in the organization."

5. Lack of Effective Messages, No Differentiation

"Our salespeople and marketing department don't talk. In fact, most of the time, they don't even like each other. Sales reps receive tons of brochures, but have to sift through it all to find the right message. And the broader the product line, the longer it takes new salespeople and product launches to get up to speed."

6. Competition—Lost Sales Opportunities

"We're getting outsold and surprised in too many deals. By the time we get to the presentation, we're in reaction mode. It seems like the competition is getting in control earlier."

7. Commoditized Pricing—We Need to Move Up the Value Chain

"Too many of our salespeople are transactional. They don't look at the bigger picture. Their attitude is to just get the deal off the table instead of growing it into a larger solution sale.

We're not building value in our solution early in the buying cycle, and as a result, procurement is treating us like a commodity in the end. Plus, for years, we have trained our clients how to buy from us at the end of a quarter."

8. Selling to the Wrong People—Politics and Relationships

"My people have taken courses on pain discovery and linking solutions, but they spend too much time doing this with people who don't really have much influence when it comes to selecting a vendor. They're not finding out who the real decision makers are. We've even been blindsided by people we didn't know were involved in the decision."

9. Silo Selling, Poor Team Selling

"Too often, we have multiple reps from different divisions calling on the same client. Our customers want one point of contact, but our salespeople at the local level can't see the big picture. Our divisions don't even talk among themselves, and that leads to conflicting strategies and embarrassment."

10. Account Selection/Segmentation Investment

"We don't know how to decide in which accounts to invest. It doesn't make sense to cover them all equally. Which ones can we dominate? Who can we grow and who do we just maintain? Which ones can we partner with? Which ones are a waste of our time? How do we decide?"

11. Poor Deal Coaching

"My salespeople are not getting the strategy help they need from my front-line sales managers. Either they don't have time or don't know how to coach deals. This affects our win rate and forecast accuracy.

We promoted our best salespeople to be managers, but the skills are different, and they get no real training."

12. Poor Discipline, No Consistency

"We've tried several initiatives in sales training and CRM with moderate success, but we've had a hard time making anything really stick."

SiriusDecisions, a sales effectiveness research and consulting firm, says:

It is all too common to see senior executives look at a longer sales cycle as something that can be controlled solely by changing internal behavior; for example, teaching their salespeople to sell more aggressively.

But in a world where buyers have more power than ever before, a sales cycle doesn't elongate because a sales team forgets how to sell; it elongates because buyers have changed the way they buy, and sales and marketing together as a tandem don't adapt.

In its "2005 Sales Benchmarking Study," SiriusDecisions defines the top five sales challenges as:

1. Need to be more effective selling to senior-level buyers

2. Need to do a much better job at generating both leads and new business

3. Need to do a better job forecasting effectively

4. Need to improve industry knowledge

5. Need to adopt a more formal "way of selling" (sales methodology)

John DeVincentis and Neil Rackham sounded the early warning years ago in *McKinsey Quarterly:* "Almost everywhere, transactional sales forces have unsustainably high cost structures; consultative sales forces don't sell deeply enough to win business; and would-be enterprise players lack the cross-functional capacity to create enough value to cover the huge costs of this approach. Most sales forces are in no-man's-land."[1]

While some progress has been made, many sales forces still face the same challenges today.

SO WHAT ARE THE ANSWERS?

Now that we have defined the problems, what are sales managers doing to solve them and achieve consistent sales performance? While we obviously haven't talked to *every* sales force, we have talked to hundreds, as well as leading consultants who have surveyed hundreds more, to identify many of the best practices in sales effectiveness.

It is helpful to think how sales executives have approached the problem in the past compared with how we must address the problem in the future.

[1] John R. DeVincentis and Neil Rackham, "Breath of a Salesman," *McKinsey Quarterly* #4, page 42, 1998.

The Evolution of Sales Processes: The Last Four Decades—From Fighting Alligators to Draining the Swamp

From the industrial revolution, when professional selling was born, to the 1970s, sales training was based on price, product, and personality. The first major change came with the birth of consultative selling for discovering needs and creating preference and action with individuals.

1970s: First Generation—Training Courses

In the 1970s, sales training and methodology consisted of a large number of small vendors in a fragmented market. The sales training at that time consisted of point solutions, mainly aimed at skills—Xerox professional selling skills, presentation skills, time management, and discovery and linkage skills from individual companies.

Prior to 1970, in addition to product training, sales training consisted largely of motivational speeches and awareness in one- to two-hour bursts, which had a wide range of effectiveness but usually a short shelf life.

1980s: Second Generation—Curriculum Coordination

In the 1980s, since the market was highly fragmented, sales managers and training executives realized that they needed more than one training course—they needed an entire curriculum of training courses. This was so especially after companies moved from selling products to selling solutions. The birth of consultative selling, linking solutions to business issues, was the standard of this decade.

During that time, vendors often would be asked to meet with their competitors to build a coordinated curriculum for their clients, sometimes internally branded under the client's label.

1990s: Third Generation—Integration

As buyers moved to companywide solutions, selling to multiple buyers on a committee required competitive and political opportunity strategy management in addition to basic skills courses of how to win individual preference.

Also in the 1990s, sales training moved to an era of tailoring and integration. Buyers wanted materials and processes customized to them and integrated into their CRM systems, training programs, and compensation plans.

Sales managers realized that if they didn't manage the interferences from the rest of the infrastructure, they would be training salespeople to do one thing while paying them to do another—with obvious dismal results.

Inconsistent attention was still being paid to adoption and change management issues, resulting in spotty execution.

2000: The Future: Fourth Generation—Perpetual Advantage

Improved metrics and visibility into the pipeline—along with integration with sales infrastructure, better deal and performance coaching by front-line managers, and a feedback system that refreshes competitive messaging every 48 hours or less—can result in a closed-loop sales and marketing system.

Only with such a closed-loop system—one that integrates sales, service, marketing, design, and perpetual innovation—can you achieve *perpetual competitive advantage.*

Only then can we lengthen the average 24-month employment span of sales executives.

Some of these are new ideas; some are not. Some of these pains have been around for a long time. So then why are they *still* pains? You already may be aware of these best practices, but the real challenge is, "How well is your organization actually *doing* them?"

PATHWAY TO PERPETUAL ADVANTAGE

In preparing for battle I have always found that plans are useless, but planning is indispensable.

Dwight D. Eisenhower,
U.S. General and President (1890–1969)

A good plan, violently executed now, is better than a perfect plan next week.

George S. Patton, U.S. General (1885–1945)

If there are gaps in your sales performance in comparison with your potential, how much change do you need? Do you need better execution, continuous improvement, or a major transformation? The answer, to some degree, depends on whether you are new to the organization, how it has performed in the past, your own expectations, and those of your management.

In talking to several executives who have successfully achieved quantum leaps in sales effectiveness, we have found that they have used similar approaches to define, prioritize, and execute the changes needed in their sales organizations.

After the sale of American Management Systems (AMS), a Fairfax, Virginia-based consulting firm, to CGI, Donna Morea was named president of the newly formed U.S. subsidiary, one of our principal Peter Bourke's accounts.

Prior to the merger, AMS and CGI had very different sales organizations. AMS was highly centralized and organized by industry—CGI was highly decentralized and organized by geography.

Donna's approach to changing the new organization to a more sales-driven culture concentrated on three legs of a stool. "We focused on (1) how we sell, (2) who we sell to, and (3) what we sell," she said.

The first focus area centered on the need to adopt consistent and proven sales disciplines across CGI-AMS (the how). Second, Donna pushed the organization to adopt a new approach to segmenting the market (the who), with the goal of focusing the majority of CGI-AMS's account management and business development resources on a smaller number of strategic accounts. Finally, she worked with her leadership team to "overlay" the geographically oriented organization structure with an industry focus—enabling CGI-AMS to articulate a clear go-to-market strategy for each of its core industries (the what).

The result was less focus on pure one-off customer consulting and more focus on their core competencies and industry solutions where they already had deep expertise and a solid track record of performance. This was more profitable and lower risk. In the "how" leg of the stool, they adopted new processes for account and opportunity management. They also redefined roles and responsibilities for the sales teams to reduce the "swarming" approach used in the past.

To make this new sales culture "stick," Morea said she had to get leadership to embrace the new vision initially on faith and ultimately through experience.

"Those were the 'noble' means," she said. "The 'less noble' means included money. We had a fund that we set aside that included discretionary money for our most important opportunities. To get the money, they had to learn and use the process and the tools."

"We wanted to inspire people," Morea said. "To sell the vision, it was really important for us to find some quick wins using these principles. It's amazing what a little bit of success can do to convince the skeptics."

"I figured 10 to 15 percent would be early believers and sign up. Then, another 60 to 70 percent would follow a win.

But there will be 10 to 20 percent who never sign on, no matter what," she said. "The 60 percent majority is made up of good people. Once good people see that you have good tools, they will behave rationally. Good people understand that good tools will help them execute. You're never going to get everyone."

Performance reviews—ensuring that sales managers were reinforcing the new culture and coaching—were introduced, and an internal coach, available at large, was added. The internal coach's job was also to monitor the forecast for sales phase changes and to make sure strategy sessions were being conducted at the right time.

The new sales culture is a success. And the company recently closed a $350 million government contract.

The first step is identifying the gaps in your performance potential and execution. On a scale of 1 to 3, rate the following pains as they apply to your organization:

Sales Effectiveness Gap Analysis (1 = Not a pain; 2 = Somewhat a pain; 3 = Major pain)			
Sales Pain			
Unclear sales process, no common language	1	2	3
Missed forecasts—Happy ears, surprises	1	2	3
Qualification, chasing bad deals	1	2	3
Selling too low—We can't sell high enough to execs	1	2	3
Lack of effective messages, no differentiation	1	2	3
Competition—Lost sales opportunities	1	2	3
Commoditized pricing—We need to move up value chain	1	2	3
Selling to the wrong people—Politics and relationships	1	2	3
Silo selling, poor team selling	1	2	3
Account selection/segmentation investment	1	2	3
Poor deal coaching	1	2	3
Poor discipline, no consistency	1	2	3
Other pains:	1	2	3
	1	2	3
	1	2	3
	1	2	3
	1	2	3
	1	2	3
	1	2	3
	1	2	3

"WITHOUT VISION, THE PEOPLE PERISH" *(Proverbs 29)*

A vision is important, but the last thing that we suggest you do is organize a committee and spend several months thrashing out a vision statement. It shouldn't be that hard.

Jeffrey Pfeffer of Stanford, in his excellent book, *The Knowing-Doing Gap*, describes mission statements as one of several substitutes for action, and they can be if you dwell on them too long. Lou Gerstner, when he took over IBM, shocked everyone when he stated, "The last thing we need right now is a vision statement." He knew that the company had to stop the bleeding first.

Bill Hybels, who has grown Willow Creek church into a megachurch near Chicago, says that "a vision is a picture of the future that produces passion."[1]

When we work with sales organizations in this area, we simply ask them for descriptive statements about their organization as it is now and how they would like it to be three years from now from the point of view of (1) customers, (2) competitors, and (3) the sales force.

After talking about each one and eliminating some, the usual revelation is "Why not?" Good visions are usually achievable, but a stretch. The next step, of course, is to translate this into goals, objectives (which are measurable and date-driven), strategies, and, finally, action items and owners.

The greatest vision statement of the last century was John Kennedy's declaration in 1961 that the United States

[1] Bill Hybels, *Courageous Leadership* (Grand Rapids, MI: Zondervan, 2002), p. 32.

would have a man on the moon and back by the end of the decade. It happened on July 20, 1969.

The purpose of this book is to help you create a vision of what you could achieve by sharing best practices of other great sales organizations, as well as the process for making it happen and a process for making it stick.

BUYING TIME FOR CHANGE—SETTING MANAGEMENT EXPECTATIONS

Every sales executive is playing a game of "beat the clock." One of the important variables in your approach to improving sales effectiveness is the relationship between the sales leader and the CEO. If the board and the CEO recognize the depth of the sales problem, and you are a new hire, you need to set expectations that this will take one to two years for a full transformation. If you can't get that commitment, don't take the job. Of course, you will have to show progress along the way.

And you can't go in and fire everyone immediately. You have to fight the battleship while you fix it. But if you don't have a firm resolution and change things proactively, the organization can absorb you like a bullet into butter.

If, on the other hand, your company is a public company and the CEO is managing the company to the analysts' expectations, or if venture capitalists are involved, don't believe for a minute that you can avoid showing quarter-to-quarter improvement. When financial strategy drives sales strategy, the result is usually short-term thinking and sub-optimization of full sales potential. This is a reality of life.

When we were selling to PeopleSoft in 1998, we met with their executive team just as a period of rapid growth was beginning to slow.

While the meeting was about sales effectiveness, we gave them this warning: " Next year, you'll grow by 50 percent, but your stock price will fall in half. And there is nothing that you are willing to do about it." They were stunned.

The reason we could make such a bold prediction is that we had seen it many times in the software industry.

The previous year, they had grown by 80 percent, but competition had finally matched their technological advantage in their core products. But PeopleSoft had planned on an 80 percent growth *again* and had planned expenses accordingly.

So, as predicted, sales grew 50 percent, expenses grew 80 percent, profits took a hit; the stock fell hard.

Most companies would die to have a 50 percent growth in the coming year and would make a lot of money. But who in an organization is going to go in and tell the analysts that their growth is going to slow next year? The hit on the stock price was twice as hard as a surprise than it would have been earlier.

Letting the analysts set your sales goals is a prescription for new horizons on your career path.

SETTING PRIORITIES

The executives we've worked with who have made dramatic improvements in sales effectiveness are able to prioritize the gaps in their performance and balance short-term quick-win initiatives with longer-term infrastructure changes.

Although sales improvement initiatives obviously can be conducted *simultaneously* rather than sequentially, in general, they approached their priorities in the same order.

You may choose priorities differently, but we share the experiences here of three successful executives who have achieved significant sales improvements as a benchmark.

Terry Turner is a veteran sales executive who has experienced changes in buying habits in three different industries—manufacturing, supply chain, and now, education. He is currently senior vice president, sales and marketing, for Harcourt Assessments.

"This was my third time transforming a sales force and each one has been different.

At Harcourt, the way the buyers buy in this industry had changed, but the sales force had not. Sales had been taking orders for existing clients on educational assessment tests and developing and informing clients about new products. The industry changed from sales to local school districts to highly competitive test adoptions for entire states—a much more complex sale for higher stakes.

In the initial assessment, we knew we needed to change the selling culture from product-driven to sales to customer-experience-driven. We were more focused on protecting turf and guarding silos than on winning or building relationships with clients.

As Jim Collins says in *Good to Great*, we had to get the right people on the bus or where we were going didn't matter. And we also had to get some people off the bus. I knew to start with sales management to have the most immediate impact. If I hired new salespeople who went to work for managers selling the old way, we would get nowhere.

I replaced most of the front-line managers with people I knew from my network who shared the same values, sales process, and hiring profile. People who are cynical or indifferent about change will kill your efforts with passive resistance or poor attitudes.

The second step was to change our sales messaging to more accurately convey our strengths, benefits, and differentiators rather than features.

The third step was to redefine our sales process to give everyone a playbook defining what a good sales effort looked like and what questions, information, and action items were needed in each phase. This training gave the reps a roadmap for managing a complex sale and the managers a common set of expectations for selling and coaching.

We also changed our team structure, roles, and responsibilities. We are blessed with outstanding products and people who have a great deal of expertise in educational testing. Many of them came from client backgrounds. Teaming them with professional salespeople to lead the team has allowed us to leverage our talents by getting the right people owning the right parts of the sales cycle.

The fourth step was to start redefining and reinforcing a new culture for selling and servicing customers and building relationships. This impacted every division of the company, so I needed upper management's support to handle the inevitable power struggles. We also turned over around a dozen reps out of about a hundred who were unable to change or grow.

In the next year, we will focus on improving the foundation selling skills of discovery, linkage, presentation, and objection handling. Now that we have the right people and the right strategies, next follows execution-level skills.

I initially set management expectations that it would take over a year to realize any progress. I gained influence and bought time with upper management when they saw the types of sales managers I brought in. Then, after the sales process training, we won several large deals where the new process was acknowledged to have played a significant part.

We are now focusing on the necessary coaching and metrics to make the process permanent."

Another example of how managers set priorities to achieve dramatic sales improvement comes from Lexmark:

When I spoke at Lexmark in 2002, I could tell that Bruce Dahlgren, the vice president and general manager, understood sales performance and how to make it happen. He knew that the strategy of building an installed base of printers—and their related supplies—needed to be complemented by unique service and solution offerings. Simply put, they had to build more value.

Lexmark was previously the IBM printer division and had remnants of that culture. But Dahlgren changed the way the company sold with new people, new process, and new positioning for his solutions. And he reinforced it with coaching.

Rather than simply moving printers and ink, Dahlgren's team focused on the larger strategy of "Print, Move, and Manage," a spectrum of industry-focused solutions aimed at helping Lexmark customers address real printing and document process challenges. That meant more consultative selling and new roles for some people.

"Turnover had been at around 25 percent before, and we kept it there for a couple of years," said Dahlgren. "But we were much more purposeful at bringing in a new profile of salesperson able and willing to sell solutions. Now the turnover rate is down to 3 percent."

With the right people and processes in place, Dahlgren turned the attention of his management team to account strategy development and coaching.

"My managers had a challenge merely finding the time to coach," Dahlgren said. "So I looked at their administrative workload and eliminated several reporting activities that weren't really needed. We had to convince finance, but it freed up the time. The other thing we did was to designate every Monday as a coaching day in the office. Each manager reviews each major account and the action items for the week compared to our plan.

We also wanted to send the message that I actually *read* the forecasts and account plans. This let them know that our focus on coaching was not some half-hearted initiative they could ignore and hope would go away."

"**At** Manhattan Associates, one of the things we've done right is that we have always had a mantra that 'everyone is in sales.' It's in our DNA—to do whatever it takes to best address the needs of our customers and to continue to deliver ongoing value," said Jeff Mitchell, executive vice president of Americas at Manhattan Associates, a leading supply-chain solutions provider based in Atlanta.

"When I began this job, other than cultivating a sales culture, my focus was probably on people first. We are a culture that believes in very strong processes, methodology, and a common language.

Now, we focus on business execution. We focus on lots of things in the beginning and middle of a sales cycle that you have to execute well in order to put you in a winning position on 'game day.'

We do manage the sales process with technology. It's important, but not one of our top three items. Instead, we focus first on our people and the domain expertise they provide to our customers; second is the value proposition our solutions provide; and third we focus on our management people who are here to ensure successful execution. Then we focus on leveraging technology to further improve and extend the capabilities and deliver for the above.

For example, before we built our sales and marketing and implementation tools, we focused on raising our value proposition to a more strategic level. You have to ask the right questions first and really understand the business problems trying to be solved. Once you get all of the questions, the tools are the easy part.

Before, the sales reps just had to get the solution consultant to the presentation. Now the sales reps do so much more in the discovery phase—leading up to the presentation—to ensure that everyone is ready for game day. The scope of our offering is such now that one solution consultant can't be expected to bring 100 percent of the domain expertise to the table single-handedly. So much of the strategy for success and overall coordination happens before the demo.

As far as coaching is concerned, we prioritize it. Most of our people have the expertise and can coach a deal, but doing it day in and day out has to be part of your culture."

EIGHT STEPS TO SALES TRANSFORMATION

1. Assessment—Where Are We Now?

There are two approaches to assessing benchmark strengths and weaknesses. You can use experience and intuition, or you can do a more formal assessment. Or, depending on the amount of time you have, you can do both.

Some weaknesses are immediately obvious to a new manager, and you can begin taking action right away. Sometimes, however, when you have been there a while, the real weaknesses in a sales force may be harder to detect. I've been in evaluations where it was obvious that the management had a gut feel for what they needed but really didn't know because they hadn't measured it.

This book should help you with an overall organizational assessment scorecard. Assessing individual sales rep talent can't really be done effectively until you have defined your ideal sales cycle and the skills and competencies that this demands.

The quickest and most effective way to start is with a win/loss analysis by an outside third party. This will give you the quickest feedback on why you are winning or losing and where your fastest returns for improvement lie. All this can and should be completed within 90 days to determine your initial priorities.

2. Start with People—Managers First

To put it simply and starkly: If you don't get the people process right, you will never fulfill the promise of your business.

Larry Bossidy and Ram Charan, in *Execution:*
The Discipline of Getting Things Done

Front-line sales managers are the key to any sales initiative. Most managers fail because they stick with poor performers too long. Without sales managers who share your vision and values and who can and will reinforce your process, new hires will be like pouring water into a leaky bucket.

Most successful sales executives have a following of loyal lieutenants whom they can call on in these situations. For those who have burned their bridges, this takes a while longer.

Once front-line managers have defined a new hiring profile for reps, they can begin upgrading the talent, replacing those who can't or won't change.

3. Next Is Your Sales Process

If you can't describe what you are doing as a process, you don't know what you're doing.

W. Edwards Deming (1900–1993),
Father of Total Quality Management

Third-party methodology vendors can give you a jumpstart in this area, but the outcome should be your own unique best-practice sales cycle for your company and your industry. Your sales technique should include the concepts from the methodology and form the basis of your training effort.

Defining your sales technique also will secure buy-in from your sales managers because it is their own work. The entire coaching discipline hinges on their reinforcement. It should be in both their performance review and comp plan, or you will get no more than a passive effort.

This can become a huge overkill project if you let it. It should be done in less than a week.

4. Positioning—What Do We Say About Us?

Would you persuade, speak of interests, not reason.

Benjamin Franklin, *Poor Richard's Almanac*

As outsiders, when we review sales messaging, we often find unfocused "me too" messages that sound exactly like the competition. Too many features, too few benefits, lack of focus on solutions for buyers, and poor differentiation— all delivered in brochure format to the sales force.

An objective, and often brutal, evaluation of your techniques in this area usually is needed to make sure that you are not "eating your own dog food." The vice president of marketing's buy-in here is essential to avoid defense and denial.

5. Creating a Winning Sales Culture—Align the Infrastructure

Priorities in this area include alignment of the new sales process with the rest of the sales and marketing infrastructure. Unless compensation, rewards, roles and responsibilities, support, and policies are aligned with the new selling process, you will simply increase frustration by training salespeople to sell one way while the rest of the organizational systems incent them to act a different way.

Sometimes your new process may drive new roles for some people. These must be defined clearly and sold internally. Finally, the whole organization needs to support a selling culture as one team. This is where the support of the CEO is not an option.

6. Execution—Level Selling Skills

Some sales managers prefer to address individual selling skills first and then move to competitive strategy. Others prefer to make sure that they are selling to the right accounts and the right people before they focus on developing the skills necessary to create individual preference. Many companies have used two different vendors simultaneously to address these competencies.

These individual-level skills include discovery, listening, probing, linking solutions to pains, vision creation, presentation and writing skills, objection handling, time management, and negotiating, among others. Who needs and who gets this type of skills training should come from the performance review, which should come from your ideal sales cycle. The application of the skills should fall out of your sales strategy for that account. The result is more realistic strategy-based execution skills training rather than generic classes.

Using a single vendor allows a completely integrated strategy and training approach. Whatever the priority, though, both skills *and* strategy are needed to identify the key decision makers and win their hearts.

7. People and Process First—Then Automate

Why is technology so low on the list of priorities? Because if you take a bad process—combined with weak people—and automate it, you will just accelerate mistakes and frustration.

Joe Galvin, of Gartner, Inc., states: "Sales culture dictates to a large degree technology adoption and that technology alone will not change behavior. . . . Sales productivity will be improved by sales technologies only when it is deployed into a sales culture of leveraging its potential."

The graveyard of failed sales force automation initiatives has taught us that refining your processes first—selling the right messages through the right people—should precede any sales force automation effort.

8. New Metrics and Feedback for Perpetual Advantage

A transformation demands sustainable change. Too many initiatives wane after the first few months. Sales messages quickly lose effectiveness due to competitive responses. It shouldn't take a year to find out whether or not a salesperson can cut it, and by the time a deal hits the forecast, it is usually out of control.

Permanent process change to get ahead and stay ahead of the competition requires faster feedback and newer metrics than ever before.

Since not all sales improvement efforts are alike, setting your priorities depends on where your sales force is and where it needs to be. Based on the successful transformations we have observed, we have built an assessment tool to help you compare your organization with the best practices of top sales forces.

CHAPTER

DEFINING
THE SCORECARD

Quality is not an act. It is a habit.

Aristotle

Once you agree that your sales force is in need of improvement, where do you start? How do you assess your sales organization in addition to just revenue? How do you identify your weaknesses?

The principals of our firm, all successful sales executives themselves, have worked with more than 250 leading sales organizations worldwide. Together, we have identified five universal areas of sales effectiveness—*Talent, Technique, Teamwork, Technology,* and *Trust*—and how they differ at each of the four levels of sales strategy: *Individual, Opportunity Management, Account Management,* and *Industry/Marketplace.* In Chapter 9 we discuss essential elements of achieving and maintaining *Transformation* for permanent change.

Although most sales organizations execute best practices in *some* areas, rarely do they achieve best practices in *all* areas. And certainly, these are *not all* the best practices in selling, but they should be enough to get you ahead of your competition and closer to your true potential as a sales force.

The result is a scorecard that we have developed to provide sales managers with a gap analysis of their organization. Through this scorecard, we'll show you how you compare with some of the best sales forces in the world.

INTRODUCTION TO SALES EFFECTIVENESS BEST PRACTICES: THE FIVE T'S OF TRANSFORMATION

Here we will briefly introduce the criteria. In later chapters we will go into much more depth.

Talent
The first step in sales effectiveness is finding the right people. Selling in a complex sale requires a unique combination of sales competencies. Most of the sales managers we talk to say that fewer than 20 percent of their salespeople can consistently manage a complex sale independently.

Most people interview based on two things: performance and personality. But there isn't a salesperson out there who can't craft a good résumé and sell a one-hour interview. So what do you look for? Every interview is a selling event. Without a good hiring profile, which has been *written and tested*, how will you know what a good sales-person looks like when he or she walks in the door? Most people who think they have a good mental picture of what they are looking for would be stunned by their inconsistencies if they actually wrote them down.

Technique

There are hundreds of companies that teach sales skills—presentation skills, objection handling, closing, etc. But the one skill many salespeople lack is the ability to effectively connect their solutions to the prospect's business problems.

In addition to a greater understanding of the client's pain, refinements and techniques continue to advance in the areas of controlling politics, competition, and the decision-making process.

Innovations also have occurred in both deal coaching and overall performance coaching, as well as in the area of forecasting.

Teamwork

The salesperson's contacts and calendar are a starting point, but they are not enough to manage an opportunity. To *lead* in a complex selling environment, you have to be able to communicate the plan *to the rest of the team*. You have to have a stakeholder analysis that identifies who is involved, what role they play, what their pains are, and how much power they have. *It's not enough for salespeople to keep it in their heads anymore.*

Also, the relationship between manager and salesperson needs to move from inspector and loner to one of coach and strategist. In the rare accounts where partnering is a possibility, the team also can include the client.

Everyone on your sales team who touches the account needs to know what's going on, what the strategy is, and must collaborate on execution and refinement of the plan.

Technology

Unfortunately, most client relationship management (CRM) applications haven't lived up to their promise—especially in the area of direct business-to-business (B2B) sales force effectiveness. And, if implemented badly, CRM technology actually can build a barrier between you and your best clients.

The first CRM applications for direct sales were contact managers, designed to capture the salesperson's "little black book" (today, it's their personal Outlook file) in case they left the company. In the complex sale, however, there is more to it than just contact information. The real valuable corporate asset isn't names and addresses—it's the customer relationships.

Nevertheless, information is an essential tool to create a better customer experience in the hands of the right talent, using the right process, with that objective in mind.

Trust

Everyone talks about "relationships," when what they really mean is *trust*. You have to build trust in your company, your people, and the quality of your solutions so that you can win repeat business with less effort and lower cost. This is the currency of account management.

What people really want is someone who knows their business. Tell them something about their company they don't know—don't just read information off a screen. You have to show the connection between your solutions and their issues and then sell up the chain of value. This is where salespeople themselves contribute their greatest value.

Partner is the most abused word in selling today. Buyers want more than lunch and a human brochure. They don't really need professional friends. What they want are people they can trust to solve their business problems. This means that salespeople need to know as much or more about their customers as they do about their own products.

FOUR LEVELS OF SALES STRATEGY

Sales strategy should fall out of marketing strategy (I think I heard this in business school), but it rarely happens to any great degree. Which accounts you invest in should be a part of your industry and marketing strategy. And an opportunity needs to be worked in light of what is going on in the rest of the account. How much time we spend with individuals should be a function of their role in the opportunity decision and their power in their organization.

The result, unless you are in a small account, should be an integrated four-level strategy that focuses every resource on your sales team and the client organization for maximum leverage. Unfortunately, though, it usually doesn't happen this way.

As we move from selling to individuals to selling to departments that have a more complex decision-making process, each of the four levels of selling strategy requires different talents, techniques, technologies, teamwork, and messaging. The outcome is a unique strategy for that account, in that industry, that leads to the final outcome—trust.

A brief definition of the four levels will help us to define one dimension of the scorecard, which we will then explore in greater depth in following chapters as we move through the Five T's of Transformation.

Industry/Market

Not every industry buys the same benefits or makes decisions in the same way. Focusing on specific industries allows you to become more consultative in your sales approach and to differentiate yourself with focused benefits, differentiators, messages, and solutions. This approach yields not only competitive advantage but also less "commoditization" at negotiating time.

Smaller companies often focus on a single industry. And the added cost and travel of a vertical approach to multiple industries necessitates economies of scale. Some companies approach this by teaming industry experts with competitive salespeople. In rare instances, extensive relationships and industry expertise can be combined in one individual—the *industry networked consultant,* the highest level of competency in selling.

Account Management

Few companies can afford to dedicate entire teams to all accounts in an industry. Choosing which ones to invest in requires purposeful segmentation and the clear setting of objectives in order to achieve incremental returns. Without a clear account plan, salespeople will wander the halls, building "goodwill" that never translates into additional revenue.

Opportunity Management

For some industries, such as capital equipment or consulting, opportunities are discrete buying events or evaluations. In others, they are opportunities to expand a flow of products through a channel, such as consumer packaged goods through a retail chain.

In either case, opportunities need to be inventoried and evaluated in light of all activities in the account *and* in the pipeline in order to combine our efforts and leverage our relationships.

Individual-Level Strategies

In larger organizations, "companies" themselves don't buy anything. Committees made up of individuals usually make decisions in a complex sale. People make up their minds first individually, and then they politically rationalize them or compromise them in the committee based on the decision-making algorithm.

Different stakeholders play different roles in the decision-making process and have different amounts of power within their organizations. Once you have determined which votes matter, you need an individual strategy to win their hearts or win without their vote. Building preference with everyone equally is inefficient and ineffective.

SALES EFFECTIVENESS SCORECARD

This scorecard is not for measuring what you *know to do*. Instead, it is for measuring your *execution* and *consistency*, for that is where sales effectiveness and competitive advantage lie. Within each cell are one or more best practices and, therefore, potential areas for focused improvement.

Once you have identified the gap between where you are and where you need to be, you must decide which areas are easy and which are hard to implement and then prioritize your initiatives.

We will discuss each column in a separate chapter. At the end of each chapter is an assessment, where you can score your own organization. (If you would like to see how your organization compares with others—you can take the survey online at www.complexsale.com.) In addition, it might be helpful to see how your sales managers and the rest of your management team would score your sales force to see if their opinion differs from yours.

In Chapter 9, we will discuss change management issues and the metrics needed to make any initiative a permanent change in process and behaviors.

Sales Effectiveness Scorecard

	Talent	Technique	Teamwork	Technology	Trust
Industry/market					
Account management					
Opportunity management					
Individuals					

SECTION II

TALENT

CHAPTER

TALENT

Take a group of ten players. The top two will be su-permotivated. Superstars will usually take care of themselves. Anybody can coach them. The next four, with the right motivation and direction, will learn to perform up to their potential.

The last two will waste your time. They won't be with you for long. Our goal is to focus our organizational detail and coaching on the middle six. They are the ones who most need and benefit from your direction, monitoring, and counsel.

Bill Walsh, Former 49ers Coach, *Harvard Business Review*

PLANNING FOR FAILURE

Many sales managers start the year with an unwinnable hand. Their CFO won't allow them to hire in advance of a year or to build a bench of salespeople within their firm.

Some sales managers don't even get their sales numbers until *after* the beginning of the first quarter. Then they have to begin hiring while carrying a full quota from the beginning of the year. And this doesn't take into account any turnover that might occur during the year.

As a result, sales managers overassign quotas to the sales reps they have in hopes that a certain number will exceed their goals to offset the bottom 20 percent who aren't going to make it, open territories that they begin the year with, or turnover they may have.

Many managers try to live with the lesser of two evils: (1) let a bad rep continue to work in a territory because at least there is a "body" there, or (2) live with an open territory that they must cover themselves. The most frequently made mistake is not trimming poor performers early enough. Not only does this demotivate the rest of the team, but it also takes the manager away from being a coach.

Some sales executives aggravate their turnover problem simply by increasing quotas every year based on what the analysts or CFO says the sales increase ought to be, with no thought to where the new sales will come from. Will these quotas come from better coverage, new products, new markets, increased prices, better margins, or an increased win ratio?

Without a bottom-up analysis of true potential, *raising sales quotas doesn't raise sales—it usually only raises turnover and discounts. This is one of the great myths of selling.* And if sales quotas are increased as a percentage of an individual's sales quota last year, then the great reward for a job well done, after the sales banquet, is an even greater quota for your best performers. How motivating is *that?*

While working for Atlanta-based Optio Software, one of our principals, Blake Batley, was asked to relocate to the West Coast to assume the newly created role of western regional director.

His challenge was to revamp the region, which had previously included only one salesperson and had never generated more than $500k in software license revenue.

Instead of managing the business for what was possible, the company was managing the business for the analysts. They put together a first-year plan to find and generate $10 million in the new territory. His tasks included finding office space, furnishing it with everything from chairs to computers, hiring ten new salespeople plus support staff, and getting them trained and up to speed so that they could produce $10 million in the first year of operation.

At the end of that first 12 months, they had a fully equipped office and a full staff. His team produced over $5 million in revenue on the $10 million quota. To everyone in the western regional office, it was considered a huge success. But, according to the analysts, it was a failure.

When financial strategy drives sales strategy, quite often the result is *planning for failure*. And if this overassignment of individual quotas results in discouragement or increased turnover in the sales force, a complete downward spiral begins.

HIRE AHEAD TO GET AHEAD

The solution is to improve our hiring and planning processes—to get the right people in the right jobs before the year begins. One best practice that we've seen in several companies is the hiring of junior salespeople who work either on existing accounts or on farming and marketing activities to learn the business and prepare themselves for territories when they open up. In my experience, we hired a number of these—about one per district—and many of them have turned out to be not only extremely successful sales reps but also vice presidents of sales and CEOs of their own companies. Without them, we would have begun the year behind the curve and would never have been able to catch up. The impact would have affected sales results and eventually shareholder value.

When financial strategy drives sales strategy, quite often the result is planning for failure.

Get a Bench and a Pool

The worst recruiting practice is to wait until you have an opening. This means that you are reacting to the marketplace and only looking through the available candidates in your area. The best practice is to build a bench within your own firm and a pool of candidates in your industry on which you can draw when you have an opening. It may take years to build this network of candidates, but it means proactively going after people and companies that may not be looking for jobs at the moment.

In our firm, it takes us about two years to recruit a principal. And we have the possibility of 100 or more at any one time who may come to work with us in the future. The building of this pool has not been an accident. Every sales manager should have a list of several dozen sales candidates within their contacts or background on which they can draw at any given time.

Recruit the Best Recruiters

The next best thing is to build a network of recruiters who are loyal to you. However, a *loyal recruiter* may be an oxymoron. And if you

The worst recruiting practice is to wait until you have an opening.

count on human resources (HR) or advertisements to send you the right candidates, you are abdicating responsibility for your own future.

If you're counting on recruiters, proceed with caution. Many recruiters try to play both sides of the fence. They may be using you as a net destination and a net supplier at the same time. You need to meet face to face with these recruiters, define your outline, and sell them not only on why your company is a good place for their candidates to come to work but also why you need to have a partnership with them. Make it clear that if they ever recruit from you at the same time they are sending you candidates, that will be the end of the relationship.

You have to be willing to share with selected recruiters the rules of engagement, including your compensation plan, competitive advantages, the direction of your company, and your recruiting process. In this way, they understand how to proceed with you and won't see it as an unduly lengthy process. The only thing that will keep recruiters loyal to you is the prospect of future business. Once they see your company in trouble and people starting to leave, un-

If you count on HR or advertisements to send you to the right candidates, you are abdicating responsibility for your own future.

less you have a personal relationship with a particular recruiter, they will start to prey on you and take people out of your organization. It's a double-edged sword they use. Don't let them use it on you.

Recruiters to Reps—Solve Two Problems at Once

Another best practice used by some organizations is to hire full-time internal recruiters. Why waste a sales headcount on a recruiter? These people *are* actually salespeople because they can go into organizations and find people who are not yet looking for a job and pull them out along with their friends.

When I was rebuilding my region, my company had a number of these (most of them were ex-military Recon types.) They made great recruiters, and most of them went

The only thing that will keep recruiters loyal to you is the prospect of future business.

on to have successful careers in sales and sales management. It was one of the best investments we ever made. Not because we saved recruiting fees, but because we got top-level talent.

All I ever saw in my recruiting efforts were A and B prospects. I wasted very little time talking to turkeys because of the efforts of these people. We were able to rebuild our region from middle of the pack to number one within a year. This is an excellent investment, but like many best practices, it requires a certain economy of scale to be able to afford a full-time, aggressive internal recruiter who is not just a paper passer.

WRITTEN PROFILES—SIGHT PICTURE OF SUCCESS

If you're recruiting, how do you know what to look for unless you sit down and define what a successful salesperson in your organization looks like? What traits, experience, skills and personality will predict success in your organization and in your industry? Unless you *write it down* and *test it* against your current performers—you're guessing. In the absence of a profile, you'll be hiring on hope. You will be opportunistic instead of purposeful. People tend to hire on hope and fire on faults—a *very* expensive habit.

Good Is the Enemy of Great

Not having a reason to *not* hire somebody is *not a reason* to hire them. The default is to keep talking or keep looking.

> A regional manager I know once hired a guy and fired him within three months. When asked why we hired this person, he replied, "I couldn't find a reason *not* to hire him, and he looked better than anyone else I'd seen." (These are two bad principles that need to be removed.)

One time, one of my sales managers said to me, "We can't have *all* 'A' players."

"Why not?" I said. "That's not true. That's a bad principle. Throw it out. You *can* have all 'A' players. I've done it three times in my life."

People tend to hire on hope and fire on faults—a *very* expensive habit.

But you have to be willing to wait for the star, and you have to be willing to spend more time recruiting than fixing problems for salespeople. Championship teams have no weak links. It's pay me now or pay me later, and I'd rather invest in recruiting than in fixing lost sales.

While at SAP, one of our principals, Jack Barr, met with sales directors from all over the country. He would ask them each to rank their current sales teams—how many A, B, and C players they thought they had.

Their categorizations were always similar. They all defined their sales forces as having some A players, some B players, and some C's. Their best performers were designated as "A players" even if they really weren't. In many cases they didn't really have *any* A players at all.

When Jack told them that they needed to hire some A's, they would always say, "We can't right now—we don't have the headcount."

"But if you have four C players right now, who you don't think will ever be A players, you *do* have the headcount," Jack would tell them. "You have room to hire four people."

As a sales manager, you have to be candid with yourself about what level players you really have. You should constantly be recruiting. When you find an A player—or someone who has the potential to become an A player—hire them and replace your C's.

You can only perform as well as the team you have behind you. If you spend all of your time coaching the C players, helping them sell, you can't be an effective manager to the rest of your team.

COST OF A BAD HIRE

It's not what you pay a man, but what he costs you that counts.

Will Rogers

One of the problems we have in business is that accounting systems don't measure the cost of a bad hire. Our accounting systems don't measure lost revenue because it never hit the books in the first place. But the cost is there; it's just invisible. Not only is it an out-of-pocket cost from lost sales, but also there are huge non-monetary costs that have an impact on the manager.

One thing is sure: Whatever the gap is between what you hire and what you need, the manager pays for in the long run. The costs incurred from hiring mistakes include lost productivity, as well as lost time for the manager and the entire sales team—not only lost sales from the poor production of that one salesperson, but also lost manager's time that was taken away from other people who could have benefited from good coaching—not to mention other losses such as angry customers, employee morale, and even missed opportunities.

Not having a reason *not* to hire someone is *not* a reason to hire them.

What did it cost you to settle for someone who was adequate if you missed the star who would have come along one month later and would have been a quota exceeder for the next 10 years? How much did it cost because you settled for someone who was adequate rather than someone who was exceptional? The principle is—if they aren't exceptional, they aren't acceptable.

Additionally, you have the out-of-pocket costs of recruiter fees, moving expenses, and training and travel to get someone new up to speed. What is the real cost? Most of the sales managers I talk with estimate the cost of a bad hire at—when they add it all up—a minimum of one to two year's sales quota. It takes three to six months to figure out if the new hire can do the job; then you may have to give them a probation period of another 90 days; and then it takes another three to six months to hire someone else and get them up to speed again.

Whatever the gap is between what you hire and what you need, the manager pays for in the long run. If your new hire is not exceptional, they are not acceptable.

Here is an example based on a salesperson with a $1.5 million quota:

	Range	Average
Initial hire period	1–3 months	2 months
Ramp-up and training time	3–6 months	3 months
Time to realize poor performance	6 months	6 months
Time to review and fire	3–6 months	5 months
Time to hire new rep	1–3 months	2 months
Total		**18 months**
Additional costs		
18-month sales quota × $1.5 million		$2.25 million
Recruiting fees		$25,000
Training		$50,000
Total		**$2.325 million**

If our accounting practices required us to take a write-off or write a check for this amount every time an employee went out the door, this would stop.

In addition to money, the other costs of a bad hire include

- Lost productivity.

- Time and stress.

- Error correction.

- Angry customers.

- Employee morale.

- Wasted support resources.

- Missed opportunities.

- Management reputation.

However, a very successful rep could produce quota for 10 years or more. How much time would you spend on a prospect that size? Why would you spend less time on a rep?

The next best thing is to figure out how much your real costs are so that you can figure out where your time is best spent. It's not only pay me now or pay me later—paying me later is several multiples of the time invested now.

Recruiting and interviewing are two of the most valuable investments sales managers can make of their time. But it has to be proactive, and it has to be in advance of an open territory or you will end up settling for someone who is adequate rather than being able to wait for somebody who is exceptional.

A colleague of ours, Rob Jeppsen, tells a story of when he was the CEO of a young technology company:

"You may only get one good shot at a particular client, and the wrong rep can blow this shot. You could lose the opportunity to do business with the client for years—if ever.

Our firm needed to hire two reps. I had the board putting all kinds of pressure on me to fill the territories ASAP. As important as these territories were to the company, we were unwilling to pay market rates.

I was told that 'good would be good enough.' As a result, I hired the best two guys I could find for the right price.

As it turned out, the two I chose were not people I would have hired if I had the option of waiting. These guys could not speak the language of our customers and drove away far more customers than they attracted.

As they struggled to succeed, not only did they cause us to lose real opportunities, [but] they [also] became negative energy sources, complaining about all of the things that were making it impossible for them to sell. This caused significant damage as other employees joined sides of management or salespeople.

Ultimately, good was not good enough, and it took us nearly 18 months to fully recover."

Proactive Sourcing

Another way to be proactive and get ahead of the curve is to nurture your network—take care of your people—and keep in contact with the salespeople who have been successful for you in the past. When you get your next sales management job, those people could be your pool. I know a lot of sales managers who have put themselves out of business because they not only didn't nurture the network, they burned bridges.

Another source is to cultivate professional organizations. That dead time during trade shows and conferences can be well spent getting to know the competitive salespeople who always assemble there.

It can be dangerous to recruit from clients, but there are times when clients can be a good source of candidates without destroying the relationship. You also can consider rehires—good people who have left you. Maybe the grass is greener for a reason; maybe it's the stuff they are spreading around over there. Good people can come back if you keep the door open.

A very successful rep could produce quota for 10 years or more. How much would you spend on a prospect that size?

Most managers, in their interviewing process, consider only two dimensions—performance and personality. If this is as deep as you look, you're not going deep enough.

There are a number of reasons salespeople fail and one of the biggest ones isn't a lack of confidence or commitment. *It's character.* And most interviewers fail to ask enough questions in this area.

In our management training course, we teach people how to drill down to character issues in addition to performance. We teach them to ask questions they wouldn't normally ask otherwise.

During one of our management training classes, one manager said, "I'm not comfortable asking these personal questions." The most recent exercise we had done in class was to study why employees fail. When we looked at the chart paper around the room, the irony was that 80 percent of their failures had to do with character issues, yet they weren't interviewing in that area.

What skills, experience, intelligence level, behavior traits, etc. will predict success? The answer is unique to you and your organization.

Your Sales Process Should Drive Your Talent Profile

The first step is to define your best-practices sales cycle—the template for an ideal sale in your industry segment. Then the next step is to work backwards to the activities, information, and strategies needed for each phase of your sales cycle.

Then work into the skills, competencies, behaviors, and experience needed to effectively execute each of these activities for each of the roles on your sales team (see Figure 4–1). The last step is to create the interview questions that help you to discover these traits—or their absence—and compare them to your profile.

One of the best books in this area is Don Clifton and Marcus Buckingham's book, *Now, Discover Your Strengths.* This is an excellent approach to identifying the characteristics that predict success.

FIGURE 4–1   Best-practice sales cycle competency model.

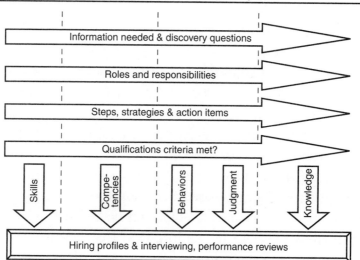

When we used Don's company in the past, we did a study of our most successful reps—hunters in the high-tech software industry—and were able to identify the most important traits to look for. In our profile, the "must haves" were that sales reps be *competitive*, have big *egos* that result in drive and ambition, and have the *courage* to overcome obstacles and initiate action from a blank piece of paper every day. We found that being *smart* also was critical. Such people make things happen rather than watch and wonder.

Other traits were either "like to haves" or fell in the category of "compensating strengths and weaknesses." However, if we didn't have the four "must haves," we knew that the person probably was not going to be successful and that the cost of hiring such a person was going to be high. We have found this to be true, by the way, of most hunters in most organizations. The four "must have" traits are necessary for competitive evaluation hunters, as we described in *Hope Is Not A Strategy*.

Hiring Assessments

To find out whether or not people have these traits, a number of companies offer assessments or surveys. Basic intelligence tests and personality style assessments are fundamental and inexpensive for first-tier screening. For complex sales of big-ticket items to committees in competitive situations, however, much more is needed.

One of the best people at defining selection profiles is Ross Rich of Chicago-based Selection Strategies, Inc. He not only knows what to look for, but he also has created a structured two-hour phone interview that listens to what the candidate says and also to what he or she doesn't say. Although these processes are not 100 percent perfect, they do help to raise red flags for your finalists. This phone interview and interpretation are fairly extensive, so most companies use them for finalists only, but they will show you the weak spots—where you should drill down deeper—before you make the expensive decision to hire a candidate.

As we mentioned, most people look at personality and performance, but there are potential flaws in both these areas. First of all, it's hard to judge past performance. How quotas are set differs from company to company. Thus, when a résumé says, "I made quota at this other company," what does that *really* mean?

One of our principals, Joe Southworth, tells a story of when he was a sales manager at a large software company:

"There was a candidate who I really wanted to hire. He looked great on paper—he had blown away his quota the previous year. I went into the VP of sales' office, excited about this new candidate, and told him about how he had exceeded his quota last year.

'Has he made quota every year for the last three years?' the VP asked me.

'Well, he's been selling for 10 years,' I said.

'But does that mean he has 10 years of experience or one year of experience 10 times?' he asked. 'We're looking for consistency and improvement. What you really want to know is, is he getting better every year or is he just doing the same thing year in, year out.' "

Two better questions to ask in assessing past performances of salespeople are

1. How did you compare to your peers?

2. Which percentile was your sales performance in each year?

You also should get specifics on *how* they overcame challenges. Take the groomed references they give you and ask for referrals to other, unsolicited references and teammates who may have worked with the candidate on deals. Their perspective on the rep's contribution and competency is usually *very* enlightening. Often their silence or faint praise speaks volumes.

Another important question to ask is what percentage of the reps at your past employer made quota every year? Many salespeople made their quota from 1995 to 2000 because they were reacting to demand in a hot market. If you didn't make quota, you were considered a failure. In other companies, only 50 percent of the salespeople made it every year. Having this metric gives you some sort of a benchmark to compare quotas.

Different industries also have different sales rhythms— the size and number of deals in a year. Some salespeople are used to a deal a day, some one per week, some one per month, and with some organizations, it's only one deal per year. Knowing what percentage of their business came from repeat orders vs. new name or competitive sales can indicate whether they are a hunter or a farmer.

Another challenge is taking transactional salespeople and putting them in a long sales cycle. Some salespeople are better at more frequent sales rhythms, whereas others are better at working on bigger deals over long periods of time.

Are Great Salespeople Born or Made?

I am often asked if great selling ability is something that people are born with or whether training is necessary. Without a doubt, there are great intuitive salespeople with innate abilities (see Figure 4–2).

Dave Sample, a long-time client of ours, now at Blackboard, summed up the problem like this: "Heroics don't scale." Yes, there are people who can do this intuitively, *but there aren't enough of them.* You have to find them *and* you have to grow them.

Not only that, but intuitive salespeople are unconscious about their competence. If your sales model is different from their experience, they may not be able to adapt because often they are good but don't know why.

So both hiring and training are important. But what can we change in a person, and what is in a person that is too difficult or time-consuming to try to change?

The nature versus nurture question has been the subject of many stories over the years, as in the movies *Wall Street* and *The Firm*, for example. In both stories, the main character was tempted to actions outside their basic principles, with grave consequences, only to find their true character in the end.

FIGURE 4–2   Are salespeople born or made?

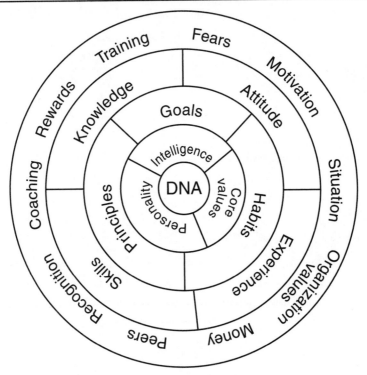

In Figure 4–2, it can be seen that there are things in a person's DNA and in their early development—intelligence, personality, core values—that are very hard to change. And a person may change behavior a little for a little while. But if that change is at odds with the person's inner fiber, eventually, they will snap back or be ineffective because their heart is really not in their actions. Thus these inner core traits are what you should really focus on in your hiring. In my experience, people usually have to bring these things with them.

The next layer out—goals, habits, and principles—are drivers of action and daily choices. If these are to be changed in a person, they need to be changed within the first 90 days of when the person is hired. The company may set a goal or principle for a person on the outer ring of the figure, but if that goal or principle is not owned in the person's heart, the result is usually a weak or false effort and ultimately, replacement.

Heroics don't scale. There are people who do this intuitively, *but there aren't enough of them.* You have to find them and you have to grow them.

Knowledge, skills, experience, and attitude are the things that enable a person to accomplish his or her goals or job. Obviously, these can be trained and managed by rewards. The rest of the figure includes the many areas management can address to direct short-term behaviors.

Notice how far inside we have placed *habits*. This is where the subconscious overrides the conscious. Changing organizational behavior often means changing individual behavior, which often takes time and consistency.

PAGE'S 10 P'S OF SUCCESSFUL HIRING

It's a funny thing about life; if you refuse anything but the best, you very often get it.

Somerset Maugham

Based on experience, I have identified 10 different elements that need to be considered when hiring a successful salesperson, sales manager, or anybody for that matter. Most of my first interviews last either 30 minutes or two hours. Before I hire a salesperson or principal for our firm,

I meet with him or her for at least eight hours—two of which are outside the office at dinner.

In the United States, HR managers are very nervous about the types of questions asked in interviews for fear of litigation. In reality, lawsuits probably are cheaper than bad hires. (A statement such as this usually sends HR managers right through the roof.) The problem is that the cost of bad hires is invisible and the cost of litigation is *very* visible. The truth is that bad hire costs, as we have discussed, are very expensive.

Each one of these elements has a number of questions that will help you to drill down past the standard questions to find the right things you're looking for. We have to get through what they've done and what they seem to be to who they really are.

Personal Accountability

As you would blame others, blame yourself; As you would forgive yourself, forgive others.

Chinese proverb

This may be the single most important element in hiring successful people. Some people would rather fix the blame than fix the problem. How do you uncover this tendency? First, it's always "them," never "me." "It's the product"; "It's my manager"; "It's support resources"; and so on. In all behavior modification—from 12-stepping to weight loss—you have to *own* the problem. Some people find an excuse, whereas others find a way.

Life is a grindstone. Whether it sharpens you up or wears you down depends on what you are made of.

68

> **O**ne researcher asked a set of twins—one a successful physician and the other a derelict—the same question: "What contributed most to where you are in life?"
>
> Both answered, "Well, what would you expect from the son of an alcoholic?"
>
> One used his background as an excuse. The other used it as a driver.

Life is a grindstone. Whether it sharpens you up or wears you down depends on what you are made of.

My favorite interview question is, "When did you become an adult and how did you know?" This will tell you when the person took personal accountability for their life.

Most successful people have an answer for this question. For some, it was a memorable event, such as the death of a parent. For others, it was a series of events, such as when they went away to college, when they got married, or when they had their first child. Or it may have been when they got their first job or when they took charge of their spiritual life.

 Joe Terry is one of our principals and one of the top 10 salespeople I have ever known. I interviewed him for over eight hours, including dinner. About halfway through a bottle of wine, I asked him the "when did you become an adult" question.

He knew the answer very clearly.

He said, "I was orphaned at an early age and was raised by an aunt and uncle. They sent me off to military school when I was a teenager. The first night there, the other kids ganged up on me and beat me with ramrods. I knew then and there that I could only look to myself."

My friend, Rusty Gordon, CEO of Knowlagent, grew up in Sapulpa, Oklahoma. He was so poor that they didn't even have a well for drinking water.

While bailing hay for horses with his father one day, his dad said, "You know, son, our plan has always been to pay for your upbringing, pay for your college, and then you would be on your own for a while and eventually we would probably have to count on you when we are older."

"Yes Dad."

"Well, son, your part of the plan is going to need to kick in a *little earlier* than we thought."

That meant not only was Rusty to go to college, but he had to support himself while there and prepare to help others.

He got himself into the Naval Academy and has since started—and run—several successful high-tech companies, never forgetting that personal accountability is a requirement for personal success.

Purpose

The secret of success is constancy of purpose.

Benjamin Disraeli

Some people are driven by sibling rivalry, others by the threat of poverty, and others by achievement. Still others are seeking a parent's approval or are driven by their own insecurity or self-image. What does this individual consider to be his purpose in life? How does this individual's purpose align with the goals of the organization? What plans has he made to accomplish these goals and fulfill this purpose? Or is the person drifting through life like the feather in the movie *Forrest Gump?*

The point is that successful people are driven by *something*. And it's usually not just the money—it's what the money brings. The point is that they are driven by a purpose and that it aligns with the job.

Principles

In matters of principle, stand like a rock. In matters of taste, swim with the current.

Thomas Jefferson

Principles are values acted on. They are shaped by an individual's personal and professional experiences. You need to know the unwritten rules that drive an individual's behavior so that you'll have an idea what they will do when you aren't watching. Does the person have a moral compass? Circumstances and temptations reveal a person's character. Is the person consistently trustworthy or completely situational? This also helps you to understand how the person wants to be managed.

This is a good place to ask the person an ethical situation question to see how they would respond. Another good question is how the person responds to problem-solving situations. What internal rules guide the person's decision-making process?

Plan

It's not the plan that is important; it's the planning.

Dr. Graeme Edwards

Some people live life; others let life live them. To achieve sustainable success, attention to detail and a high activity level must be personal habits. Are your candidates consistent in their work habits? How organized are they? Can they handle multiple tasks at a high rate of speed?

Do they know where they want to be? Do they know where they are today on that plan? Can they articulate their plans to get to where they want to be?

It has been said that "if they are failing to plan, they are planning to fail." Plans change, but how will they manage their territory and their accounts if they have no plan for themselves?

Preparation

The will to win is important, but the will to prepare is vital.

Joe Paterno

Preparation includes education and past employment from the candidate's résumé. When I ask candidates, "What have you done to prepare yourself for leadership?" I often get a blank stare. Sales is a *leadership* job: you have to be able to get people who don't work for you to follow you.

How well your candidates have researched and prepared for the interview is one of the best indicators of how well they research and prepare for sales calls. Do they know your company's history, culture, financials, and issues? Did they at least read your website?

Passion

If you aren't fired with enthusiasm, you'll be fired with enthusiasm.

Vince Lombardi

Passion represents enthusiasm for the work itself, for service, or for the people or organization and its vision. The first sale must be in the salesperson's heart. If they don't buy it, they can't sell it. If they don't have a contagious conviction about what they are selling, neither will the buyer.

At some point candidates need to pick up the special nature of your company and turn from buyer to seller. If they don't, they are not passionate about working for your company or not passionate at all. "If you think this is just another place to work, you should just work at another place."

Performance

The closest a person comes to perfection is when he fills out a job application.

Stanley J. Randall

No one works in isolation in today's business environment. Ask about the *source* of the candidate's past sales success. How important was the product? Was the market hot or not? Did the candidate rely on other members of their team to carry them? Are they used to one big deal or several small ones? How closely did they work with their manager? Was the candidate a team leader or a loner? Some people are better at different types of sales. This is why a salesperson can be good in one company and not another.

For salespeople, quota performance is an arbitrary measure. Two questions to help put this in perspective are

1. What percentage of the sales force made quota every year?

2. How do you compare with the rest of the sales force? Top half? Top 10 percent?

Personality

Be yourself is the worst advice you can give some people.

Tom Masson

People buy from people they like and people they trust. Will their interpersonal skills and chemistry wear well over time in your industry and with your clients? Are they sincere? Empathy is a necessary component of consultative selling. The people they interact with over time will be able to tell if they are sincere.

Will they fit in with your team culture? Ask yourself, "Would I like working with them?" Also consider their presence, image, and the way they dress. We make choices when we put on different clothes. It is important that they know how to dress when dealing with clients in different industries—especially if they are going to be selling to executives.

Ken Cornelius, president of Siemens One, says that he and his executive team have a simple test that many prospective hires who did well in the initial interviews fail in the end:

"After the interview rounds, we ask each other:

1. Would you like to be stuck on a deserted island with this person?

2. Would you leave this person alone with your CEO for an hour?

If the answer to either of these is 'No,' we don't hire them."

Clients and prospects can discriminate for whatever reason they choose, and they'll never tell you the reason. Remember that most candidates can sell a one-hour interview. Look past the charm to the character.

Several years ago, we were thinking about adding a new principal to our firm and had zeroed-in on one particular candidate.

Everything checked out. He had a great résumé and a great personality, but one of our principals—Liz McCune—sensed something "phony" about him, though she couldn't put her finger on it.

Our president, Brad Childress, and I decided to have a get-together by playing golf with this guy all afternoon. We had a wonderful time.

But afterwards, at dinner, his personality changed dramatically. He was abusive to the wait staff, being very short and rude when he spoke to them.

We realized that—in a social setting—this particular candidate had a hard time getting along with people he considered to be lower on the totem pole. The only way we could find this out was to get him in a situation where his guard was down.

He passed all of the one-hour interviews. He was very good at peer-to-peer relationships. But only in a social setting did we see that he was unable to interact with people lower in the organization than he was.

And in a complex selling environment, you have to be able to get along with everyone.

Practical Intelligence

To be conscious that you are ignorant is a great step to knowledge.

Benjamin Disraeli

Howard Gardner, who developed theories on multiple intelligences, says that there are at least seven kinds of smart. *Practical intelligence* extends beyond the amount of education and training the candidate has. Although knowledge is important, being able to apply it—through mental quickness, political savvy, and common sense—is essential.

Cultural literacy—knowing a little about a lot—is also necessary to be able to communicate with all types of people with varying interests. A critical type of intelligence for salespeople is *discernment*—the ability to assess multiple complex situations and determine priorities of action. Like the old vaudeville routine, can they keep multiple plates spinning in the air without dropping any?

Several years ago, Carolyn, the wife of one of our principals, Joe Terry, was studying to learn American Sign Language (ASL). One night, Joe was helping her review by calling out words for her to sign. When he called out the word *smart*, she signed *several* words. When Joe asked why there were so many signs for this one word, she explained, "In sign language, *smart* is actually *three* different words."

The amount of education or training someone has, or *book smarts*, is represented by one sign. *Street smarts*, which indicates that someone has common sense and can build relationships with a wide range of people, is represented by a different sign. And the word *wisdom* is a third, completely different sign.

Different roles require people to be different kinds of "smart." A good accountant, for example, needs "book smarts" but doesn't necessarily need "street smarts" or "wisdom" to be successful. But good salespeople, on the other hand, have to be all three kinds of "smart." They have to be well trained and educated, be able to read their surroundings and relate to people, and have the wisdom to apply this knowledge to be successful in complex situations.

Perseverance

> *I remember thinking . . . about the story of Thomas*
> *Edison's early attempts to come up with the right*
> *material for a light bulb. He had tried a thousand dif-*
> *ferent elements, and all had failed. A colleague asked*
> *him if he felt his time had been wasted, since he had*
> *discovered nothing. "Hardly," Edison is said to have*
> *retorted briskly. "I have discovered a thousand things*
> *that don't work."*
>
> Robert E. Kelley, *How To Be a Star at Work*

Successful people don't run from challenges—they redouble their efforts. If the door is closed, they find another door. Does the candidate have the ability to stay the course despite unexpected obstacles? What obstacles have they overcome in the past? If they haven't had any failure to date, how will you know how they will respond when they inevitably experience some?

The challenge here is that perseverance can actually work *against* successful salespeople in the area of qualification. No one wants to be seen as a quitter, but the best practice for individual salespeople is to choose the right battles and to qualify out of lost causes early. The question is, "Do you have a defined set of criteria for knowing when to hold 'em and when to fold 'em?"

A useful exercise that we use in our management classes is to take each of the 10 P's and rate your top three performers and your bottom three performers in a job category to see the relative importance of each attribute to that specific job.

Start Performance Management in the Interview

How long does it take to do a performance review? The answer is six months to a year because the first step in managing performance is to set the standards, values, tolerances, and expectations. You should give your candidates the performance review form and set their expectations as part of the interview process.

New hires are like wet cement. You can mold them and shape them early, but as time passes, habits form—both good and bad. After 90 days or so, their attitudes begin to calcify to the point where it may take a jackhammer to change their bad habits.

But how is the performance review actually handled in most cases? Performance reviews are seen as a necessary evil from HR, often written by HR, and often don't include the behaviors, skills, and competencies needed to perform the adopted sales methodology. They are often seen as just checkboxes to get the HR people off your back.

If the performance review doesn't include the sales methodology, then perhaps it *should* be ignored. However, if performance management is driven by the ideal sales cycle, it can be a very constructive performance coaching tool that actually should be reviewed on a quarterly basis rather than annually. This allows sales managers to coach not just deal competence, but the other factors of overall performance such as character, chemistry, competence, commitment, communication, and cognitive skills.

The time to start this process is in the interview itself, where expectations about how you want things done in your organization can be set early.

Talent Scorecard

Best Practice, Talent	Importance Degree of Importance (1 = low 10 = high)	Execution			
		Agree but we never do this	We sometimes do this	We often do this	We do this consistently
Individual					
We have written, tested profiles for each sales position.					
We have questions, assessments, and an interview process that produce consistent performers.					
We generally have the sales talent in the right roles.					
We have sales performance reviews that include our sales methodology and are introduced during the interview process.					
New managers are trained how to hire effectively.					
We have a training curriculum, built on our best practices, that includes skills, opportunity strategies, and account management.					
Opportunity Management					
We have junior salespeople ready for territories when they open up.					

Best Practice, Talent	Importance	Execution		
	Degree of Importance (1 = low 10 = high)	Agree but we never do this	We sometimes do this	We often do this	We do this consistently
We have a pool of candidates in our industry on which we can draw when we have an opening.				
We have full-time internal recruiters.				
We have a high win ratio in head-to-head competitions.				
Account Management				
Our customer service people consider themselves part of the account sales team.				
We have sales reps and managers who have earned trusted advisor status with their clients.				
Industry/Market				
We have industry knowledgeable sales consultants available to our sales team.				
We are recognized thought leaders by the customers in our industry.				

81

SECTION III

TECHNIQUE

CHAPTER

TECHNIQUE

Never mistake motion for action.

Ernest Hemingway

Jim Dickie is a partner in CSO Insights, a sales consulting practice that surveys hundreds of sales organizations every year and publishes an excellent benchmarking study. In their *2005 State of the Marketplace Review* of 1,040 firms, he says that only 23.3 percent of companies spend more than $2,500 per year training their sales forces. And this includes *all* types of training.

On average, this represents the expected value generated by one rep *in about two hours*. And yet 84.5 percent of reporting companies in the study stated that their sales methodology either had a noticeable or significant impact on sales performance. It seems that additional investment in training would yield significant returns. But only a third of reporting firms said that adherence to their sales methodology is either structured or optimized.

Inspect what you expect. Defining a formal sales process and/or investing in sales training has little residual impact if it is not reinforced and enforced. Higher quotas and higher quota attainment do not appear to be the result of defining processes, but of using *them.*[1]

In *Hope Is Not A Strategy,* we detailed two sales processes that are best practices in the complex sale: The R.A.D.A.R.® (*R*eading *A*ccounts and *D*eploying *A*ppropriate *R*esources) methodology for winning competitive opportunities and the T.E.A.M. (*T*otal *E*nterprise *A*ccount *M*anagement®) process for managing strategic accounts.

So that this book is fully self-contained, this chapter not only will review but also will focus on advancements, refinements, new developments, and the impact of the up-and-down economy on how salespeople sell in each one of these processes. Rather than address the R.A.D.A.R. process in detail, we will provide a summary here and an in-depth appendix at the end of the book. Because readers have asked for more detail on the T.E.A.M. process, we explore it in more depth here.

We will then focus on best practices in coaching the process and increasing forecasting accuracy.

R.A.D.A.R.®: THE SIX P'S OF OPPORTUNITY MANAGEMENT—SUMMARY

The R.A.D.A.R. process is used for managing complex sales evaluations by committees. It brings together the

[1] Jim Dickie and Barry Trailer, *Sales Effectiveness Insights—2005 State of the Marketplace Review* (Boulder, CO: CSO Insights, 2006), pp. 164–165.

best ideas in consultative selling, competitive selling, political selling, and team selling. It focuses on selling strategic benefits to strategic buyers and technical benefits to technical buyers. This methodology allows salespeople to control the competition, politics, and the decision-making process to increase their chance of winning.

Additionally, R.A.D.A.R. is a dynamic planning process to help you develop strategies and plans early in the sales process and revise them late in the process, when things turn emotional and political. In fact, how well and how quickly you review and revise your plan is more important than the perfection of the initial plan.

1. Link solutions to the prospect's *pain*—for greater value.

2. Qualify the *prospect*—for best resource utilization.

3. Build competitive *preference*—by differentiating your solution.

4. Determine the decision-making *process*—for driving strategy.

5. Sell to *power*—by finding the key to buyer politics.

6. Communicate the strategic *plan*—for effective team selling.

An opportunity management process is for winning competitive evaluations either in existing accounts or in new-name prospects. Investing in account management is done to make opportunity management either easier or unnecessary by winning the evaluation before it begins.

T.E.A.M.: THE EIGHT "ATES" OF MANAGING STRATEGIC ACCOUNTS

When managing large, strategic accounts, you want to maximize the revenue, relationships, and "reference-ability" potential based on the account segmentation you have determined is best for your company strategy.

The methodology that follows includes the best practices that we have seen and produces an account management map to effectively sell between the sales. These elements are not sequential but rather form a planning loop—which should be reviewed at least quarterly—and are often executed simultaneously.

Penetrate

Penetrating an account may be achieved in several ways: through winning the first piece of business in a competitive evaluation, as a result of demand-creation selling rather than demand-reaction selling, through another business partner or division, or through corporate headquarters that results in a client-vendor relationship of some sort.

Once you have penetrated the account and won the business, you have to be ready to deliver. The first piece of business is usually based on price, proposal, and product.

Demonstrate

Clients often take credit for successes and blame vendors for failures. You must *demonstrate* your value by going back to the client and documenting the effects of having chosen your organization and solution. What outcomes, benefits, metrics, and gains have been achieved by having used your firm in the first place? Clients rarely write a paper that describes how wonderful a vendor is. You have to do that yourself. But make sure that you can back it up. And if you haven't delivered value, then that becomes your strategy—account repair.

Evaluate

Segmenting accounts for future investment is a critical step in account management. It's a waste of time to try to partner or earn preferred partner status with everyone. Some company cultures are that of a commodity buyer. They always have been and always will be, and it will only change at the top. In this case, you need to *evaluate* whether you should invest additional resources in this account in an effort to gain preferred vendor status or should you stay on a transactional level.

> I once had an opportunity to sell to Pepsi, one of our competitor's best customers. They called me and said that they wanted a national account agreement with us. I was young and excited and flew out to meet with them. I asked them, "What does it mean to be your partner?"
>
> They said, "You have to offer us the same discount your competitor offers."
>
> In return for the discount, I asked them if they would put us on a short list for future purchases so we wouldn't have to fight for every piece of busi-

ness. I also asked them to promise us a yearly meeting with their IT department. They said "no" to both. They wanted a 50 percent discount just for the privilege to compete.

I walked away.

We decided not to be their partner, but to go after other pieces of the business at the local level. As it turned out, our competitor didn't spend much time on the account because the discount was so great. We stayed at the transactional level and did fine. If corporate couldn't help us, they weren't going to hurt us.

Radiate

If you decide to invest in growing an account, you need to *radiate* to power sponsors early in the game. Radiate from those who know you and like you to those who *need* to know you and like you—*before the next formal buying process breaks out*. Use one executive sponsor to take you to another. Ask each who else in his or her area/industry you can be doing this for.

Unfortunately, too many people either get too focused on delivery of the first project to radiate out or they have the hall pass and get stuck in their comfort zone, calling on people who are already sold. In addition, sales "hunters" hurry down the road to the next prospect company because what is qualified for long-term account management is not qualified for a short-term quarterly-driven "hunter." This is why "hunters" usually don't make good account managers.

Collaborate

One way to elevate your value from commodity to strategic is to *collaborate* with the client on product or strategic initiatives. This requires working on issues other than just your product. It may mean logistics, marketing, codesign, new markets, integration, or innovation.

This is a very powerful model for raising value and has led to technology tools for product configuration, change orders, design, and collaboration through an entire supply chain.

I meet a lot of sales managers on airplanes. I remember flying into Minneapolis, sitting next to a sales manager for a paper company.

Of course, I asked him, "Isn't it hard to sell a commodity like paper these days?"

He responded, "I have about 1,200 other salespeople in the commodity division. What I do is co-design specialty papers for clients with unique needs. I'm meeting with 3M tomorrow to collaborate on papers for products that we will both produce two years from now. The margins are much higher.

Likewise, later that year, I sat beside a carpet salesman, flying into Washington, D.C., who was meeting with Marriott Corporation to design special carpets for hotels they would build throughout the world over the next few years.

"It's the only way we could get out of the commodity business," he said.

Elevate

Elevate your executive relationships to trust and your solutions to the strategic.

ELEVATING TO STRATEGIC PAIN

A few years ago, one of our principals, Jon Hauck, was in a presentation with a sales rep who was presenting to the president of a major division of MCI and two of his lieutenants.

The lieutenants had prepared and coached them for the presentation, which was to last an hour. This was the big day! They thought they knew the president's key issues, which could be addressed by their slick sales dashboard that would provide significant visibility into the forecast.

But just 20 minutes into the presentation, they could see that the president was tuning out. Though the rep was doing a very nice job, unfortunately, the only heads that were nodding were his and those of the lieutenants. Jon reached over, closed the laptop, and asked the president if visibility into the forecast was what *really* concerned him most.

"Yes," he said. "But you've missed the issue. In the Telco space, forecasting revenue is not about when it's *sold*, but when the switch is *turned on*. That's what I need to forecast. I already know what my sales are going to be."

With that, they immediately changed direction and probed a little deeper into his actual issue.

He cordially explained it, and they artfully created the linkage from the benefits of their solution to solving his true pain. This took about 13 minutes.

When they told him they could do what he needed, the deal was done. He told his sales operations manager to get with them, define the scope, and tell him how much to spend.

Two weeks later, they had a contract for over $500k.

STAY INVOLVED—DELIVER
WHAT YOU SOLD

Early in the implementation of the State of Texas payroll system, Joe Terry, then the salesperson on the account, ran into a potential two-week delay to get the system installed because the client's database manager was going to be on vacation and would miss the installation training class.

The next class was not to be held for another month, but the database manager refused to change his vacation schedule. At the project level, the project manager had chosen to simply let the delay stand.

Joe went to the deputy controller and explained the hidden cost of having the 30 people on the project team stand idle for a month while the project was on hold: $720,000.

That was a pretty expensive vacation.

The controller interjected himself in the process to prevent the delay, but just as important, Joe gained trusted advisor status with the controller. This access proved to be crucial as the project ran into the normal problems that can sometimes escalate out of control.

Many salespeople reach the executive level to get the sale and then leave the support team to work at the lower levels of the account. Sometimes the problem is actually the customer's. By maintaining the access and relationships at the executive level, after the sale, Joe was able to save the customer from themselves without going over the project team's head—he was already there.

He elevated the relationship to trust by staying involved in delivering what he sold and saved the executive from embarrassment.

HELP THEM DEFINE
THEIR REAL PROBLEM

One client executive of Deloitte's came to them and said, "We need to do something about increasing revenues."

At the time, Deloitte had developed a process called a Value Map that allowed them to break processes into different areas. When they mapped the client's problem to the Value Map, they saw that none of the projects the client wanted done addressed revenue at all.

The real initiative was that the client needed to cut costs. The client was asking Deloitte for the wrong thing.

> **When dealing with someone from a strategic standpoint, before you ask, "Are you doing the *thing* right?" you have to ask, "Are you doing the *right* thing?"**

Dominate

Dominate doesn't mean manipulating the client. It means changing the client's decision-making process to give you the inside track as a preferred vendor. This will occur only because of lowered risk through superior performance and relationships. It means building company-to-company trust, in which the client doesn't have to put you out for competitive evaluations every time, or if they must, you get the inside track or high ground before it begins.

Inoculate

To *inoculate* means to provide solutions that are "sticky"— solutions that have a high switching cost so that moving away from your organization is not easy. This moves you out of the commodity relationship into a symbiotic relationship where you need each other.

It also means building allies and listening posts for competitive intrusions because competitors will try to penetrate your account the same way you did in the first place. If you do account management well

What is qualified for long-term account management is not qualified for a short-term quarterly-driven "hunter."

enough, you may not have to do opportunity management at all, or if you do, you are well established on the issues and have powerful people who prefer you before a formal buying process begins.

REFINEMENTS AND ADVANCEMENTS

Coaching: The Key to Organizational Sales Discipline

Additionally, the salespeople who grew up in the 1990s are now sales managers. In many cases, we've taken our best salespeople and made them managers with little preparation. You can't afford to take two years to send them away to earn an MBA, and that wouldn't work anyway. In MBA school, they teach you how to be a vice president and how to analyze problems—not execute solutions.

What sales managers are really asking for at this stage are tactical skills and training for new managers on how to hire effectively, coach performance, weed out weak people, and develop future leaders. Otherwise, you are taking salespeople—whose strengths as salespeople not only may *not* work for them as managers but might actually work against them—and promoting them.

As managers, they then clone more salespeople with bad habits. At the same time, there is a whole new generation of salespeople out there who not only need the fundamental skills of selling but also need to understand the complexities of committee sales and major accounts.

Sales managers have an even more difficult challenge than others because the skill sets they need to coach *their people* are much different from what is needed to coach a *deal*, yet they are intricately entwined. The trap is that many managers become "inspectors" instead of coaches, doing deal reviews without asking the tough questions or adding value by improving the strategy.

Many sales executives are figuring out that they can no longer grow with the sales techniques that have gotten them to where they are now. While coaching deals might have been an option in the up economy, it is essential in a down or flat economy. The new managers who were salespeople in the up economy may never have learned how to really analyze and coach a competitive deal.

Today's Economy Affects the Way We Sell and the Talent Pool

One discovery we've made since the last book is the impact of an up economy and a down economy on the way sellers sell and the way buyers buy. The change in the economy has had a significant impact on the talent pool for salespeople and managers and the competencies they bring with them.

In the boom economy of the 1990s, a lot of bad habits were allowed to continue. As Jim Dickie, of CSO Insights, says, "In a hurricane, even turkeys can fly."

There were some poor role models among salespeople and managers and a lot of mediocrity in selling that still resulted in high sales because it was a seller's market.

These poor selling habits came back to roost when the market turned down. Many of the "one-year wonders" could not compete effectively in the new, tougher selling environment.

Several things began to happen. First, in the consulting world, salespeople had gotten used to proposal lobbing—

answering 10 RFPs, throwing them over the castle wall, and winning two, which was enough to keep people off the bench.

In the down economy, there was no longer enough business to keep consulting firms busy. Our phone began ringing off the hook as those firms realized that they needed to get more competitive and better at selling in order to win their share or even grow.

Many consulting firms began to develop sales processes, hire outside business developers, and focus on sales training. While making significant improvements, one challenge still remains in the consulting industry—and that is the lack of an overall sales hierarchy and sales management and accountability infrastructure, as well as a hiring profile that leads to a competitive culture.

The Lost Art of Prospecting

In the rest of the sales world, we began to get a lot of calls from sales executives who said, "You told us how to win deals, but we don't have enough deals to work on in this economy. Our pipelines aren't full enough."

Salespeople had forgotten how to prospect because they didn't need to for the past 10 years. Instead, they had let marketing handle this responsibility. They had forgotten how to pick up the phone and call a stranger or felt that they were past that in their careers.

At the same time, executives today are barraged by more people than ever trying to get to them—through e-mail and voicemail—so the clutter is even greater. We work with a number of firms to help them refocus their prospecting efforts and demand-creation selling: how to get to executives, how to do research before you get there, and how to identify their top two or three issues so that the chances of a voice-mail or e-mail creating a 30-minute meeting actually may have some chance of working.

The goal is to identify an executive who will sponsor a project and find a budget in the absence of an evaluation.

Procurement Grows Stronger—Commoditization

Another impact of the down economy is that procurement has gained more power. Procurement has always been a stakeholder, with greater strength in government than in the commercial sector. In the down economy, though, its strength has grown as efforts have increased to drive cost out of companies so that they can compete globally.

As a result, sales cycles, after the vendor-selection decision, have developed a *second crucible* for the approval cycle, which can be as difficult and lengthy as the process for winning the business itself. This means that after earning the business, we need to better equip our sponsors with a business case for the economic buyer.

The best practice is to become more proactive in this phase of the process rather than leaving it up to the client.

As the economy declines, companies focus on cost cutting rather than on innovation or revenue-generating activities. This has been reinforced by the global impact on prices from low-cost producers in Asia. As a result, procurement has more power, even over strategic purchases.

By nature, procurement is inclined to ignore value and focus on price. In fact, procurement managers are measured and rewarded for it. The end users are the ones who understand value. This is why procurement people try to separate you from them at the end of the sale. Commoditization is not only a sport to these people, it is also a way of life. Even when they understand strategic value, they are trained to ignore it—at least in front of you.

They will say such things as, "I don't know. You all look the same to me, but you're more expensive. What can you do for us on the price?" Left unchecked, these people will drive you to the door and then catch you by the coattails.

Also remember that there is a mirror image of client relationship management (CRM) for procurement people called *supplier relationship management* (SRM). Also called *strategic sourcing,* procurement best practices call for segmenting suppliers into different categories based on the importance of their value and the availability of substitutes.

This gives them four segments:

- High importance, low substitutability—*strategic*

- High importance, available substitutes—*preferred vendor*

- Low importance, low substitutability—*manage risk*

- Low importance, available substitutes—*commodity*

Many procurement people actually know the difference between buying strategic solutions and buying commodities, but they often pretend that you have less value to their firm than you do. Moreover, ERP systems for the bigger firms now provide procurement with information about global spending with your organization, as well as prices your firm has quoted elsewhere in the world. This is information the sales reps themselves often don't have. And information is becoming available through consultants about what prices were quoted to other firms.

While they focus on price, you must continue to refocus on value. They will argue over thousands while you may be making them millions. Where do you find this value? From the initial discovery and linking your solutions up the value chain.

At the same time, the attorneys are paid to imagine the worst possible outcome—litigation—and many want to prelitigate in the contract. You need the powerful executives who will be *using* your products and services to explain what is normal risk, what can and cannot be achieved, and your competitive differentiators and their value. Without their involvement negotiated early in the sales cycle, you will find yourself in a battle of wits with lawyers and procurement—unarmed (see Figure 5–1).

In our negotiating classes, we teach that the best practice is to bargain *early* in the sales process, while you have something to trade, to get your sponsors to advocate for you with procurement. Why would they do this for you? Remind them that their future depends more on the success and risks of the project or product than on negotiated price—and that a degree of partnership will be necessary for the future give and take.

Remind them that the relationship includes the negotiation. And you can't go from partnership to abuse and back to partnership—especially if you have taken all the margins out of the deal. If they don't agree to arbitrate value on your behalf later, you might seriously consider not investing further resources if you see a price beating coming in

FIGURE 5–1   The approval process—the second crucible.

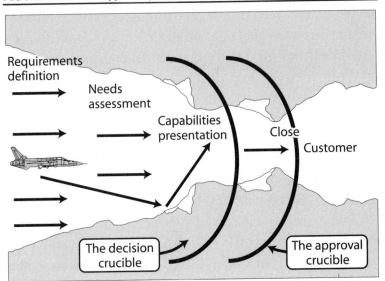

your future. We have a commodity buyer who has called us every year for six years. We have fired the buyer as a prospect every year. We know the company won't pay for value in the end. We spend a little time to see if the company's culture has changed or if the company representative person has enough power. If not, we move on.

Understand your value, continuously refocus the discussion around it, and *never go to procurement alone*. (Although you actually may have to physically go by yourself, your sponsors should have paved the way and be in the background, supporting your value.)

Value-Based Account Segmentation
There are many ways to segment accounts in a market. Since you cannot and should not invest in all accounts

equally, deciding in advance which accounts will yield the greatest return on investment of additional time and resources is obviously a key decision. Traditionally, among the factors usually considered are historic revenue streams, reference-ability, account profitability, and quality of the relationship.

In *Hope Is Not A Strategy*, we defined six levels of buyer-seller relationships that have evolved over the years (see Figure 5–2). On the right side of the figure we define six levels and roles of sales talent that can be committed to an account. We also identify six different types of buyers based on *the way they buy*.

For firms selling value-added solutions rather than commodities, a developing best practice is to allocate resources and define strategies based on the way the customer is willing to pay for value. For example, if you commit partnering resources to commodity buyers, you will partner yourself

FIGURE 5–2   Six generations of buyer-seller relationships.

Value-based
segmentation & strategies

Buyer	Company-to-company trust	Seller	Value & margins
High trust	Partner	Partner	
Sponsor		Demand creator	
Solution	Collaboration, differentiation, value	Consultative seller	
Competitive		Hunter	
Repetitive	Lower cost, easy to buy	Farmer call center	
Low trust	Commodity	Teller, Web	Commodification

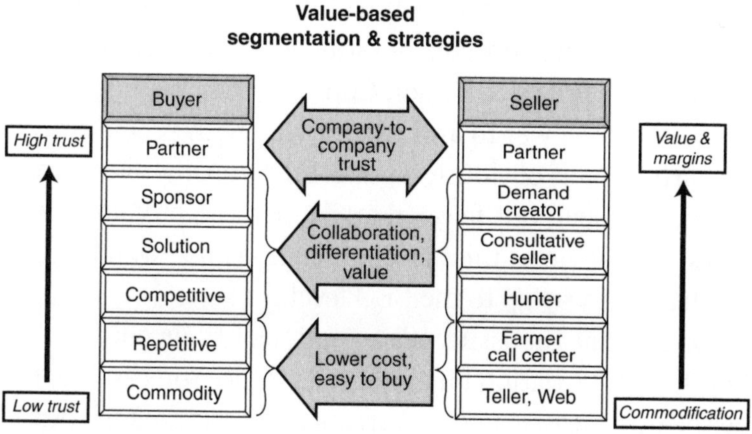

broke lavishing attention on firms that will still put you out for bid.

For commodity buyers and repetitive buyers buying noncompetitive add-on sales, the strategy is to make it easy to buy and keep the cost of sales low using the Web or telesales. For buyers who buy in competitive evaluations, "hunters" who can manage and win these political battles are a necessity. If you put your "farmer" up against their "hunter," you will get creamed.

A solution buyer will allow you to collaborate, understand his or her needs, and co-develop a customized solution with a consultative seller. This obviously takes a significant investment of both time and talent. A demand creator can find a dormant business problem and create a vision of a solution. Then he or she finds a sponsor who is a change agent with enough political power to drive the proposal into buying activity.

A danger exists in investing these resources and value-added strategies if you are then going to be shoved down to procurement, only to have the value stripped out of your deal. The gamble is that you will have gained enough differentiation through collaboration that you are uniquely qualified to provide the solution and that your sponsors have enough power to arbitrate for you with procurement.

Partnering is obviously a powerful company-to-company business model, but fewer than 10 percent of your candidates can achieve this special relationship, which must reach all the way up to the CEO level.

Size is not the issue. It's a matter of their culture. It's how the organization buys and sells value. You can judge it by the way the organization treats other vendors. If the organization doesn't partner with anyone else, it isn't going to partner with you.

ROI Alone Is Not Enough

In the area of pain, one observation we've made over the last few years is that in a down economy, return on investment (ROI) alone will not compel an opportunity to close. Many training programs that address selling to executives focus on the financial benefits exclusively by teaching how to calculate the benefits of your solution and then calculate a stream of cash flow and an ROI on that assumed cash flow.

One of our clients was selling new point-of-sale systems to Wal-Mart. In their eight-store pilot, they determined that, using their systems, Wal-Mart could save $2 million a year, spread over eight stores, or $250k per store per year.

But, since they didn't link the savings to any strategic opportunities for Wal-Mart, it was no surprise the pilot went on for two years with no closure.

In the grand scheme of things, they failed to recognize that $250k per year per store wouldn't get anyone's attention.

For a company that does almost $300 billion a year, a $250k annual savings is merely a rounding error.

There weren"t enough zeros in their value proposition to be compelling.

ROI is now a requirement to get in the game. It is no longer a differentiator but a satisfier. We can look at forecasts and tell you which deals are going to stall. Where your solution is not linked to compelling value (emotional and political pain associated with a powerful person), it is probably not going to close anytime soon. Logical arguments alone are insufficient. It takes a crusader—a powerful person inside the organization who wants it to happen—to get resources from other projects or money in the budget and assume the risks of any new procurement.

Jack Barr tells a story of when he was competing to win the Hershey account while at **SAP**:

"I was involved in a very competitive situation, selling manufacturing/order processing software to the Hershey Company in Pennsylvania.

My competitor and I were called in to present to the executive committee. Before the meeting, I went through my presentation with my internal coach to make sure it hit the mark. My coach told me that, as a company, Hershey was very focused on *children*.

Milton Hershey, the company's founder, never had a formal education. To him, providing this opportunity to others was an important priority. He and his wife established a school for orphans and made sure that the town of Hershey had the finest elementary and secondary schools possible. Every year, millions of dollars are donated to the Hershey

Foundation, which continues to fund the orphanage and schools.

'Everything is about the children when it comes to Hershey,' my coach said. 'A percentage of our net profit goes to the Hershey Foundation every year. So before we do anything for the business, we always ask ourselves, Will it benefit the children?'

Based on that conversation, I added one slide to my presentation that figured how much our solution could save the company in inventory costs. I was able to show them how much this savings would add to their bottom line and how many additional millions of dollars could be donated to the Hershey Foundation, by the Hershey Company, as a result over the next five years.

Though my competitor's solution would also have saved them in inventory costs, he didn't present it with the same linkage to the emotional and personal benefit to the Foundation that I did. The feedback I got, after I won the deal, was, 'Jack really understood what we are all about.' "

Someone (or a group of people) with power needs to see the vision and opportunity of how a solution can help his or her organization defeat the competition, enter new markets, regain and/or capture customer share, produce significant shareholder value, or provide a competitive advantage to the company.

Gary, a sales rep reporting to Jerry Ellis, one of our principals, was selling planning solutions systems to a large health care organization.

Together, they had gained access to the company's vice president of finance, Bruce, who reported directly to the CEO.

While meeting with Bruce, they asked him *why* he was planning to replace the current use of Excel in his organization with a new budgeting and planning solution. Bruce responded with a long list of reasons why the current use of Excel required was overly time-consuming and caused his team to work long hours, including weekends, to meet the continually changing requests of senior management.

After listening to Bruce's explanation of the frustration the current approach caused his team, Jerry said, "I know senior management is concerned about your team's quality of life, but the tool you are using now gives them the information they are asking for. I doubt they will spend $250k just to make your life easier. How will you justify our solution to them?"

Bruce then explained the real strategic justification he would use for the new system: It would allow them to move newly acquired health care facilities into their overall process faster, which would ultimately save them money faster and enable them to more quickly add to the overall bottom line.

This team knew that without linking the purchase to more strategic pains, Bruce would not receive funding approval. Through this questioning, they confirmed that the solution could be linked to the strategic gains of powerful stakeholders and that the project sponsor could articulate linkage between their solution and these strategic gains.

Relationships Alone Are Not Enough, Either

Another flaw we see in some organizations is that they focus on building preference through linking solutions alone or through relationships alone. If you focus on linking solutions alone, you ignore the power of relationships. There are over 50 ways that people build influence with each other.

Stephen Covey, in his book *The Seven Habits of Highly Effective People*, refers to this as "building emotional bank accounts with each other." I'll trust you for two reasons: (1) because you're an expert, you're reliable, you can solve my problems, you have the company and the functionality behind you, and I know you'll get the job done, or (2) because we went to school together, you know my family, you're my friend, you know my business, you've worked with us before, and I know you'll work night and day to get things done for me.

But what if it's a tie? If it's a tie, I'm going with my friend. Whenever the product or solution is a tie, relationships are the differentiator. But when it's a high-risk situation and I'm betting my job or the company on it, I can't go to the committee or my management and say, "I prefer this company because the salesperson is my friend." I have to provide a business case for why I prefer you over another company.

Likewise, many salespeople are counting on relationships alone. They are professional friends, or they think they can get by on their personality, by entertaining their clients, and by being grateful for the business. This just isn't enough anymore. Buyers want better business values.

About a year ago I spoke with a trade association, and the head of procurement for a major electronics retail organization was there. He said something to the effect of, "People call on us all of time saying that they want to be partners and build a relationship with us. Yes, we do have partnerships. We have about 3 strategic alliances and 12 preferred vendors. But everybody else is a commodity to us and we put them out for reverse auctions. People come by and say they want to have a relationship with us. Frankly, we're just not that lonely."

Frankly, we're just not that lonely.

While there are some lonely buyers out there, they still have to build business value for having selected your company. In relationships alone, you can linger, but you can't last. On solutions alone, you may get outsold while you have a superior product if you don't have strong enough relationships.

 Our principal, Joe Terry, was working a big deal once where the divisional vice president had the power of a "gorilla" in an algebraic democracy. His vote counted "the sum of all votes plus one."

Joe had a good relationship with the vice president, based on previous experience, and assumed that he had a preference for our firm.

But in the executive presentation, the vote came down to five for Joe and one against him. After some research, Joe discovered that the vice president was also personal friends with the competitive salesperson and played golf with him every week.

Turns out, the vice president, who we thought was our ally, was the one vote for the competition.

Joe knew that he had the superior solution, so he went to the vice president and said, "I know you have a difficult decision to make because you are also friends with my competitor."

After talking with Joe, the vice president agreed that Joe's solution would achieve his strategic objectives and that it would be very risky for him to try to achieve those same objectives with the competitor's solution.

Joe suggested that the vice president abstain from the vote and allow the other five people on the committee to make the choice. This way, he could tell his friend, Joe's competitor, that he had been outvoted.

This proved to be a way for the vice president to save face with his friend *and* to reach his business objectives by going with the better solution.

Joe won the deal, and the vice president became one of the biggest supporters that drove the initiative throughout the company.

The key to this strategy was to recognize that personal preference was only good if he could also

solve the problem. Had Joe not had a relationship with the vice president, he probably could not have had this type of discussion with him. And if he had not had a superior product, relationship would have not been enough to win the deal.

DEFINING YOUR BEST PRACTICES SALES CYCLE

The Six P's methodology includes the elements that need to be attended to in order to win a complex sale. We teach them sequentially, but in fact, salespeople use them simultaneously.

Once you qualify an account with a dispassionate process, you use a combination of a *stakeholder analysis* and a metaphor of the sales cycle which we have named the *canyon and crucible* (see appendix Figure A-1). The stakeholder analysis identifies each buyer's pain, power, part, and preference in order to determine a plan to win the heart of each of the key voters or live without it. This process is overlaid with the canyon and crucible, which is a chronologic assessment of the dynamics of changing issues and decision-making politics as they go through a competitive evaluation. Combined, we've put a time dimension on the sales cycle.

The best practice in the industry today is to take your sales cycle and define it in terms of the *phases* that are unique to your company and your industry. Salespeople tend to do the right things in the sales cycle, just not always at the right times. And timing is critical. How you coach depends on which phase of the sales cycle you are in. In general, we want salespeople doing things earlier than they have been doing them before. The other reason that phases are important is that they match your forecasting process.

The Sales Cycle Coaching Template—A Vision of Victory

The first thing we do with a client is take the company's sales management team and a selected number of the company's top salespeople and identify, by phase, what an ideal sales cycle looks like. What does a vision of victory look like at each step along the way?

Information drives strategy. We start by defining all of the coaching questions managers will ask during the sales cycle to see if they have included the right activities in the sales cycle that are necessary to answer those coaching questions.

Then, by phase, what are the desired outcomes, questions to ask, information needed, roles and responsibilities, qualification criteria, and action items (with due dates and owners) for each of those phases? The result ends up being a template of an ideal sales cycle from which managers can coach and compare. Because they built it, they own it, and it is tailored to their business. It is then provided to all salespeople so that they won't feel ambushed when the tough questions are asked.

The R.A.D.A.R. six P's methodology, combined with your sales process, creates a best practice sales template unique to your organization. The purpose of a sales cycle template and a coaching session is to (1) guide the sales team on *how* to execute these action items most effectively, (2) identify *who* to focus your efforts on, and (3) explain *why* the salesperson should do certain activities or *what is the risk of not doing* the activity.

All a salesperson has is time, and the decisions he makes on that time are critical to his success. You can't really "make time," and you can't really "save time." All you can do is change the quality of time spent.

The idea is to have one sales cycle for your company for each market segment or industry. By the way, it shouldn't take that long to build this. We've seen companies spend over $1 million and months with consultants to have this built. Then it sits in a binder without training or execution.

The challenge comes—and where many of these projects fail—in the action items, questions, anticipated risks, politics, and potential objections. Most plans also don't take into account a thorough transition to post-sales team members.

A best practice sales cycle should be built in three days for less than six figures. For Apple Computer, we built eight of these—one for each industry—because the solution sets and buying processes for each buyer in each industry are different.

The way you sell to government is different from the way you sell to higher education, which is different from how you sell to health care. You may have a different buying cycle for a different solution set or industry. But once it has been developed, it should become the template for sales execution and coaching for your salespeople and managers.

FORECASTING IS NOW STRATEGIC

Under the Sarbanes-Oxley Act of 2002, sales forecasts are now a serious issue in U.S.-listed companies. Companies have to be compliant and more transparent to stockholders. As a result, boards of directors want to know what sort of analysis is behind the sales forecast.

If the CEO says that everything is going to be okay and then gets embarrassed at the end of the quarter because some deals slipped and didn't close, investors get surprised and now file lawsuits. It happens about once a quarter, and the result is a stock price that can fall 10 to 40 percent. These are high stakes for a weak forecasting system.

Why Forecasting Doesn't Work Well

One source of sales discipline is the forecast itself—especially for product-oriented companies, where the revenue is recognizable when the sale is made. But most forecasts aren't forecasts in the first place. Instead, they're "past-casts," looking in the rear-view mirror at what has happened to date.

If the purpose of the forecast is simply to predict revenue rather than to manage and coach the pipeline, then it fails to reach its potential. In reality, many deals are already out of control by the time they hit the forecast and become visible to management.

In our experience, most forecasts don't separate the issues of *if* and *when* you're going to get the business. The flaw lies in the nature of competitive evaluations. Most CRM systems simply have line-item lists of opportunities, close dates, dollar amounts, and some sort of A-B-C or 50–70–90 percent ranking.

This is actually a percentage of expected value built on the confidence level of the manager, which may come close to the total company forecast by the law of large numbers. In reality, though, you don't get a *percent* of a deal. *You either win it or you don't.*

And we have seen newspaper article after newspaper article in which companies have a bad quarter attributed to "several deals that didn't come in," and their stock has fallen as much as 10 to 40 percent in a given quarter. These aren't forecasts; they are simply wishes or guesses. Using a CRM system to automate them is just adding up *bad numbers faster*.

The closer you get to winning, the closer you actually get to losing because of the crucible effect defined in *Hope Is Not A Strategy*. As committees get closer to making a decision, politics erupt, the decision-making process breaks down, the issues change, priorities change, and the competition makes counterattacks once it realizes it is looking at 100 percent of zero.

Most forecasting systems are not tied to a methodology. They don't reflect your strategy or the buying process of the buyer. Most sales reps are too close to the action, and their judgment is clouded by wishful thinking. So they don't ask the tough, critical questions that challenge their strategy for fear that they will spoil a good forecast.

This is the sales manager's job. It's too important to delegate.

The best practice is a forecast that includes a line item but through which a manager can click and drill down to the decision-making process, politics, stakeholder analysis, source of urgency, action items, and value proposition to see what your true chances are of winning.

Then, if necessary, the manager can generate a phone call to the sales rep, which will be shorter and of greater value. Forecasts not built on methodology are a pack of guesses on which you bet your company every quarter.

Only by a forecast built on a detailed analysis of the account, reviewed in multiple coaching sessions by a front-line manager, the sales team, and perhaps some certified deal coaches can a sales manager sleep soundly at night.

Forecasting—*If* and *When* plus *How*

The best practice is to imbed methodology and sales process into your forecasting system. Although this is a best practice, we seldom see it used. Recently, we finished this process with Harcourt Assessment. Scott Sciotto, a sales manager there exclaimed, "At last—a methodology combined with a forecast system."

There are two obvious benefits to this. We see people all the time who understand the six P's as their *sales process*, still using A-B-C and 50–70–90 percent as their *forecasting technique*. But using phases *alone* fails to recognize the *competitive risk* in each deal. In a forecast, we need to know not only *when* the deal will happen but also *if* we are going to win it. Lumping the two together results in unpleasant surprises (see Figure 5–3).

FIGURE 5–3 Forecasting—separating *if* and *when.*

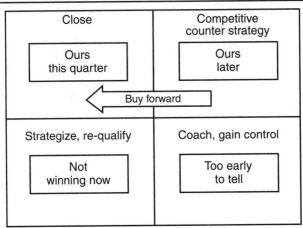

As a salesperson, I hated my manager's quarterly question of, "Is this deal going to close?"

My answer was always the same: "Are you asking me if I am going to win this deal at all, or am I going to win the deal this quarter? That is really two different questions."

Forecasting using the law of large numbers has flourished to the detriment of quality forecasts at the front-line management level.

In addition, salespeople hide deals off the forecast so that they can turn them in at the end of the quarter and be a hero. Often they are awarded a bonus for this, which encourages bad behavior.

The Next Generation of Drill-Down Forecasting

While many sales managers have embedded their sales methodology into their CRM system, new "on demand" Internet technologies have significantly enabled the integration of methodology into the forecasting system. This can

118

now be done without requiring any programming and while maintaining necessary security by keeping the data inside your firewall.

The success of Salesforce.com in penetrating larger enterprises has validated this approach. The ease of integrating CRM, forecasting, and remote coaching now allows for technology-assisted deal coaching and a new level of teamwork between sales rep and manager.

Technique Scorecard

Best Practices, Technique	Importance	Execution			
	Degree of Importance (1 = low, 10 = high)	Agree, but we never do this	We sometimes do this	We often do this	We do this consistently
Individual					
Salespeople effectively link our solutions to the buyer's pains.					
Our salespeople have the individual skills necessary to create preference for us.					
Our salespeople are able to develop value propositions that link into strategic value and emotional issues for powerful people.					
Opportunity					
Salespeople understand political power and allocate resources to winning the votes that matter.					
Salespeople effectively qualify *out* of deals they cannot win.					

Best Practices, Technique	Importance	Execution			
	Degree of Importance (1 = low, 10 = high)	Agree, but we never do this	We sometimes do this	We often do this	We do this consistently
Everyone on the sales team knows his or her role and responsibility and understands the account and opportunity plan.					
Managers know how to effectively analyze and coach competitive deals.					
Account Management					
We consistently meet customer expectations.					
We have a best practices account management cycle.					
Salespeople know how to get to executives and know what to say when they get there.					
Industry/Market					
We have a best practices sales cycle, defined by phase, for each market segment.					
We have industry-focused solutions, messages, and expertise.					

SECTION IV

TEAMWORK

TEAMWORK

Individual commitment to a group effort—that is what makes a team work, a company work, a society work, a civilization work.

Vince Lombardi

Talent wins games, but teamwork and intelligence win championships.

Michael Jordan

Everybody sells. Everybody either sells or "unsells" their company and its services with every action they take every day. From design to manufacturing to shipping to legal—everybody sells and has an impact on the company's revenue and therefore affects the company's livelihood. Some people just don't realize it. Those who don't are myopic in their view and perhaps should work somewhere other than your organization.

Obviously, this attitude starts at the top with the leadership of a company and whether or not it has a sales culture.

One by one, industries are starting to realize that they need a selling function. Ten years ago it was consulting. Before then, you couldn't use the "s" word in any of these firms. It was "business development."

Now, even law firms and medical clinics are realizing that they need a sales function—that business just doesn't come to them fast enough to fulfill their potential and that even they need to sell value and avoid commoditization.

But not everybody ever imagined that they would be in sales, need a sales training class, or have anything to do with sales. Most universities not only don't teach it, but most business schools consider it a pedestrian activity (although over 20 million people in the United States alone are employed in sales and probably at least as many throughout the rest of the world).

When we work with firms that are trying to change to a sales culture, the first thing we have to do is take away the old stereotypes—the negative images of selling—and replace them with a vision of selling that is not only acceptable but also worthwhile. Not that the negative images of selling are undeserved. There are a lot of bad salespeople out there.

Most of the bad images people have of salespeople, however, come from those who tried to sell them one thing, one time, and didn't care about their repeat business. Overselling, high-pressure selling, and all the sleazy images we have usually come from this experience.

But if we define selling in such a way that it's earning the client's business by solving his or her problems and serving clients in such a way that they never have a reason to go to anybody else, then most people find the definition acceptable. If we can define selling as outserving and out-solving the competition, most people would accept that—and that's basically what it is.

If you don't earn business in such a way that you can meet or exceed your clients' expectations, you're not really a sales team; you're a sales-prevention team. Systematically, you will inoculate your customers against doing repeat business with you.

The real test of selling is whether people will buy from you the second time. You have to do more than just satisfy the client—you have to ensure the client's return.

Real profitability lies in the second, third, and fourth sale and beyond because that is where the cost of sale is lowest and your pricing can be higher because you have lowered risk and delivered value.

TEAM SELLING

As companies have moved from selling products to selling systems and solutions, their sales efforts have moved from single sellers, who wear all the hats, to sales teams. Team selling consists of two to two dozen people selling to a committee of two to sometimes 200 buyers.

Many sales opportunities will bring a sales team consisting of an account manager, a product specialist (or several), an industry specialist, a technical specialist, a service team, and an executive or two. Since your systems and solutions may now touch multiple departments and, therefore, multiple buyers, all these people may be selling to a committee of buyers.

In team selling, each one of these specialties requires different talents, personalities and competencies, and each team member has different roles and responsibilities.

Soccer or Silos—None of the Above

In some companies, the roles and responsibilities of a sales team are clearly defined. In other organizations, including many consulting firms, such roles and responsibilities are not well defined. (One partner described his company's sales effort as being like five-years-olds playing soccer. We all run over here and kick the ball, and then we all swarm over there and kick the ball. If we score, we all take credit, and if we get scored on, everybody runs away.)

The real test of selling is whether people will buy from you the second time.

Other firms are so large—and have grown by acquisition—that they sell in silos. Multiple sales reps are often calling on the same account. They rarely talk to each other to share opportunities and contacts and, as a result, quite often end up competing with each other within the same account.

Siemens is a huge multinational company. Actually, in many ways, it is over a dozen companies, each with billions of dollars in sales.

Numerous clients buy from multiple divisions of Siemens—each of which has a separate sales force. This is normally not a problem until the client wants an integrated solution.

To present one face to the client and handle internal issues and communications, Siemens created a separate sales organization called Siemens One, headed by Ken Cornelius in Atlanta.

It was especially effective when the Transportation Security Agency (TSA), after 9/11, needed to increase airport security screening. This meant (the acquisition of) new systems, hardware, technology, and lighting, as well as consulting services.

Siemens One was able to coordinate the sales efforts of several of its divisions and produce a single-vendor solution. Its competitors offered partnerships and coalitions of multiple vendors.

The pain was strategic, and the problem was urgent. Dealing with a single vendor reduced risk and increased accountability in a solution where the political benefits went as high as world peace.

They got the business. They were not the low bidder.

"This approach and success has been repeated dozens of times on large, complex deals for Siemens," said Cornelius.

Likewise, on a global basis, many times the account is handled by the local country. The result is pricing that varies all over the board for the same business. There is also a lack of synergy in the sales effort, where many times, multiple opportunities could be combined to outflank the competition.

Joe Terry was coaching deals for a client in London and was conducting a strategy session on a $2 million deal for a big-five consulting firm.

Everything had been agreed to, and the contract was waiting for signature. They broke for lunch and returned to hear the salesperson say, "You're not going to believe this, but our U.S. salesperson in corporate just closed a deal selling a worldwide license for $450,000!"

The U.S. salesperson, with no visibility into the bigger picture, had cost the company millions of dollars in revenue from a prospect that obviously had a high likelihood of buying for hundreds of offices across the globe.

Poor negotiations? Maybe. But the real problem was the lack of teamwork and communication.

One of the first military principles of strategy is concentration of force. Unless an entire global sales team is coordinated and has a unified account strategy, the competition will have a significant chance of defeating you piecemeal. Additionally, procurement departments can outcommunicate sales teams in some situations and shop the same business around the world to get the lowest price. This not only leaves money on the table but is embarrassing to the high bidder.

In order to be most effective, teams need clearly defined roles and responsibilities as to who will do the prospecting, who will lead the account strategy, and who is responsible for providing product information and presentations. In fact, the best strategy is to map your organizational chart to the client's organizational chart so that each person on your team knows which person on the buying committee he or she is responsible for and has a strategy to win that person's vote.

At the same time, one of the first principles of best practice is *clearly defined account ownership*. Whether you have one owner for an entire global account really depends on your size and strategy and whether you have invested in those resources.

Companies that sell in silos should pick one leader of the account. That leader is given control and accountability over that account, and everybody else selling in that account is a member of that team and accountable to that leader.

Other companies define account management as simply caretaking, coordinating, or communicating. They define relationships as being friends, giving favors, and showing appreciation. All this is fine, but we define account management as allocating resources in the most effective way to achieve the greatest account potential whether it is a partnership, dominating the account, or just maintaining it.

> In team selling, the biggest challenge is moving individual salespeople from loners to leaders.

From Loners to Leaders

When it comes to managing a complex, competitive sales evaluation, the best practice is one opportunity, one owner. That way, you may be wrong, but you'll never be confused.

And confusion probably will cost you more deals than commitment to a single strategy.

In team selling, the biggest challenge is moving individual salespeople from loners to sales team leaders. Salespeople, by nature, are loners. As they started out in business, working for a smaller company without division of labor, they **A plan needs to be short enough that the salespeople will use it, but it also has to be powerful enough to win.** may have had to wear all the hats. Good "hunters" tend to be independent sorts anyway, but as they move to team selling, their job is to lead a team. The strengths that made them good as an individual may work against them in this regard—the first of which is communication.

Salespeople who keep the plan in their head have a hard time leading a team. *In order to lead a team with a plan, you have to write it down,* and many salespeople don't like to write. And most have short attention spans. For some reason, they would rather *talk* about a deal six times than *write* it down *once*.

Salespeople are drivers. They work at a high rate of speed and many of them at low attention to detail. Many deal in relationships rather than analysis. In order to get them to lead a team, accountability and discipline need to be driven from two sources: management and the teammates themselves. *The vehicles for doing this are the forecast and the strategy coaching session.*

Make the Pie Bigger First—You Can't Split Zero
Major enemies of teamwork in many firms include split policy and fighting over account control. One of the

biggest myths of selling and barriers to effective teamwork is a CFO's opposition to "paying double" commissions—especially for global account managers. This is a misnomer, but once this catch phrase has been set, it's difficult to change.

Paying more commissions for additional people on the sales team, whether they are global account managers or industry specialists, is simply a greater investment in the account in order to achieve greater returns or volumes.

The real question is whether the benefits of having additional personnel on the account will yield a return to justify the initial expense. We teach people that if they can't see their way to greater volumes, better margins, or a lower cost of sales through less competition, then they shouldn't invest in account management strategies for that account in the first place. Instead, they should pursue the business at the individual opportunity level or as a commodity through the Web or through bidding.

Often times, fights over revenue credit and commissions end up meaning that sales teams don't even pursue the business because they think that it's the other person's account. The deal falls between the cracks, or they step on each other in front of the customer.

The answer is a strategy that settles upfront what the split credit is and who's going to contribute which effort. If need be, the possibility should exist of paying additional commissions. But get the business and make the pie bigger first.

One of our principals, Phil Johnson, was selling software to Amoco Fibers and Fabrics, an Atlanta-based subsidiary of Amoco, whose corporate headquarters are in Chicago.

He asked them if Chicago would be involved in the deal, and they said, "No," so he chose not to contact his guys in Chicago. He didn't want to get them involved because he didn't want to split the deal with them.

In the end, Phil won his deal. He sent over a contract on Friday afternoon. But on Monday, Amoco called and said they couldn't sign it. Corporate headquarters had already signed a deal with his competitor for *three* sites—one of which was Atlanta.

Though Phil won his deal, he lost in the end because he didn't communicate with the team in Chicago. He didn't help them win, so they ended up losing the deal altogether.

STRATEGY SESSIONS—WHEN DO YOU WANT THE BAD NEWS? WHO DO YOU WANT IT FROM?

The difference between amateur strategists and great strategists is their ability to test the plan before the battle begins. Great generals look at both sides of the battlefield. Great chess players play from both sides of the board. Pool players and chess players can see their strategy three and four moves out.

The difference between amateur strategists and great strategists is their ability to test the plan before the battle begins. Great generals look at both sides of the battlefield.

Before every major investment of time and resources in an account—or move to a different phase of the sales cycle—there should be an investment of time by the sales team in a strategy review session. A strategy review session is not an exercise for the salesperson to sell the team on why he has a good strategy. It's an opportunity to get the bad news early from your friends who want you to win the deal. It's a test of your plan. Everyone—especially the plan owner—has to leave their ego at the door.

Leaders let everyone know what their role is in the execution of the sale, when each action item is due, and who is accountable for the results. Without a strategy session of this nature, you're not a team leader—you're a loner. And ultimately, you're probably losing.

You can ignore a strategy and *hope* to win. In fact, you can win without a strategy at all—it's called luck. (Don't pay for luck. You can get luck cheaper on the Web.) If you want salespeople who *make things happen* through a team, though, they have to seek out bad news, blind spots, and assumptions early.

If you get bad news early, there are two things you can do: you can either withdraw from the account or change your strategy and actions. But bad news late is no good because you don't have time to change, and you have spent your resources. The cement has set.

Until now, the people who have not had a voice have been the teammates—the product engineers and specialists—because the power in most sales teams lies with the salesperson or the account manager. But the product engineers are great sets of eyes and ears and can actually build better bonds at the lower levels. They are sometimes able to get information and actually validate a strategy and a buyer's preferences when the salesperson has been screened.

The Blue Angels have made several documentaries about how they are so effective flying wingtip to wingtip—at the speed of sound—and how they manage to stay alive during these incredible aeronautical maneuvers. After every show or training exercise, they have a nameless, rankless debrief.

One of the principles we learned from our friends at Afterburner, Inc., a high-impact training firm that simulates fighter strike missions and teaches teamwork at the same time, is that it doesn't matter *who* is right but *what* is right.

It's not important to defend your strategy; it's important to seek out criticism because, for pilots, when they're not right, they're usually dead wrong.

Similarly, the support people who are in the account after the last sale also have great contacts. If they're not included, you're missing a great source of information and access. These people need to have a formal way to critique the account plan—especially the

It doesn't matter who is right but *what* is right.

sales engineers, who are going to have to go in and give the presentations. If they don't understand the plan, the stakeholders, the messages they are supposed to deliver, or the strategic pains they are supposed to link into, you are not going to get a very effective competitive presentation.

I'm a Veteran—Why Do I Need a Coach?

If you go to a professional golf tournament and stand at the practice tee, you see Tiger Woods with his *coach*—as well as most of the top golfers. The golfers themselves are the best in the world and are all qualified to teach.

Why do they need a coach? Because the unconscious competent does things by reflex and needs an out-of-body observer to pick up their flaws. The conscious competent needs to build consistency. The conscious noncompetent needs technique. And they all need the discipline that a coach provides.

Top tennis players have coaches, top track stars also have them, and they are very highly paid for the value that they bring. Sales managers need to make coaching a priority part of their job because *competitive advantage comes not from awareness but from the consistency and discipline that tools and coaching bring.*

Sales Managers—Too Busy to Win

Reinforcement and adoption of any process or initiative depend on the buy-in and consistent discipline of the front-line sales managers. They always have, always will. If this is so obvious, then why have so many client relationship management (CRM) and sales automation efforts failed from lack of adoption?

If front-line sales managers don't buy it, they won't sell it. If they don't enforce the discipline necessary to adopt a sales process or technology, it will join the graveyard of failed initiatives.

Buy-in requires involvement. Getting sales managers trained first and involved in the design of the coaching template not only makes buy-in more realistic but also prevents the sales managers from sitting in the class like prisoners with their arms folded. They need to be team teaching with the instructor, linking each teaching point into a real deal that happened in their area.

Buy-in may not be as big of a problem as sales managers *finding the time* to coach—or, in reality, *making* the time to coach—because any quality improvement process requires a shift in time utilization from inspection and error correction to error prevention. Until processes are in place for error prevention (coaching and strategy sessions), managers sometimes have to make time for both—growing the deal and growing the rep. Until they make the shift to growing the rep to gain control early, however, they will always be behind the curve.

If front-line sales managers don't learn how to leverage themselves through coaching and strategy sessions, they can never really manage more than three reps at a time.

One of the first things we do with managers is to evaluate the *quality* (i.e., who takes up time, is it proactive or reactive, what is urgent/important) and quantity of their time. Of the 168 hours per week, we identify the 15 biggest uses of their time and then ask them to tell us how much time should be spent in each area, including personal time. Then we have *their managers* identify their ideal time-allocation picture for a week. This in itself is very enlightening.

We then ask each manager to track the actual expenditure of time for a month. The results usually identify several things: Sales managers are too busy selling *for* the bottom 20 percent of their salespeople who can't manage a complex sale. Almost every sales manager I have spoken with in the past 10 years admits that their bottom 20 to 25 percent of reps can't manage a complex sales cycle effectively and probably never will be able to, yet these sales managers still carry a full quota for these salespeople.

In addition, we find that sales managers often are heavily involved in the last 20 percent of the major deals because of the rise in power of procurement departments. In this phase, the buyers are often better at buying than the average salesperson is at selling, so managers need to get involved in the negotiations.

These two forces draw sales managers into becoming the salesperson themselves or out of coaching the middle 60 percent, where their coaching abilities would allow them to *leverage* themselves and increase their win rate. Delegation of high-stakes deals is difficult. But if front-line sales managers don't learn how to leverage themselves through coaching and strategy sessions, they can never really manage more than three reps at a time.

So forecasts end up being bad because coaching is bad because hiring is bad. To fix the problem, we have to start at the very beginning.

Coaching Done Badly

What are the flaws in coaching? One of the biggest flaws is *premature prescriptions.* The salesperson has worked the deal for six weeks, and the coach has all the answers in six minutes. Salespeople just love that.

Another flaw is *stealing the deal*—taking it over—espe-

Strategy sessions are a labor-saving device. The time saved by not selling to the wrong accounts, not selling to the wrong people, and not doing the wrong action items to win will more than pay for the time investment.

cially in front of the prospect. Once a sales manager has stolen power from the rep in front of the prospect, the manager has it forever. By the time this has happened several times, the sales manager is no longer the coach but a glorified rep with a bunch of juniors.

A jellyfish sales manager who listens to a strategy review but doesn't challenge assumptions, create what-if scenarios, identify blind spots, or suggest ideas provides little value.

Getting the entire account team involved, even if by teleconference, results in more eyes, more information, and therefore a better plan. Often the technical teammates form strong relationships with evaluation committee members and can provide great insight into the sales plan. Excluding them is a mistake.

The best practice coaching style that achieves critical thinking while leaving ownership with the salesperson is the Socratic technique of using questions that prompt thinking rather than statements that prompt defense.

Obviously, in losing situations, documenting lessons learned is more productive than fixing blame and pouring salt on the wound.

Manager—Walk Your Talk. Be Prepared

Another flaw is not reading a prepared account plan or strategy document before going to the coaching session. If managers will read the input or sales plan that they have asked the reps to prepare, coaching sessions can be cut in half because the rep doesn't have to spend the first hour telling the story.

Nothing offends sales reps more than taking the time to fill out a sales plan that a manager has asked them to complete, just to have the manager *not read it*. If the manager *has* read it, however, he can quickly move to value-added comments about strategies and assumptions.

It is interesting how salespeople and sales managers always seem to find time to try to "fix the deal" at the end, attempting to correct all the mistakes that were made in a 9- to 12-month sales cycle. But they don't have time to conduct strategy sessions along the way to avoid chaos at the end.

When do we find time to have strategy sessions? With teleconferences and Web meetings, it is easier now than ever before. *Strategy sessions are a labor-saving device.* The time saved by not selling to the wrong accounts, not selling to the wrong people, and not doing the wrong action items to win will more than pay for the time investment. The return on time invested in strategy sessions is anywhere from 2:1 to 10:1.

We've turned millions of dollars worth of deals around in strategy sessions with our clients and have seen them work. But it has to be a matter of discipline. Lexmark does it every Monday. Some companies have strategy sessions at each change of phase in the forecast. Other companies simply say, "No review, no resources." If it's not worth 30 minutes of your time to review the strategy with the team, why is it worth 15 hours of their time to travel across the country and look unprofessional?

The main reason that salespeople should have a strategy session is because they want to win and will have a better plan and a more committed team if they have invested the time to lead.

Enemies of Teamwork

For some companies, the biggest barrier to success is themselves. Their culture and values are so rotten inside that when you leave their building, you just want to take a shower. They can't partner with anyone else because they can't partner with themselves.

If this is your prospect, you should seriously consider whether the company is worth your time in the end. If there is a project involved, it probably won't be successful. If it is the company you work for, you probably won't be successful. Leave. Fast!

It's not worth the money.

Top 20 Enemies of Teamwork	
Personal agendas	No compromise
Insecurity	Weak links
Misaligned goals	Glory stealing
No trust	Blame fixing
Favoritism	Overemphasis on compensation
Finger pointing	No vision
Rumor mongering	High turnover
Poor leadership	Constant reorganization
Selfishness	Carrying weak performers
Internal competition, silos	Cynicism

These are the activities that are the sand in the gears of a successful team. They destroy trust. Use the preceding list to evaluate your own company's team behavior. Use it to evaluate your customers to see if you really want to sell to them. Then evaluate yourself to see if you have engaged in any of these activities. The best salespeople build strong teams inside their own organizations to get things done for their customers.

Teamwork Scorecard

Best Practice, Teamwork	Importance	Execution		
	Degree of Importance (1 = low 10 = high)	Agree, but we never do this	We sometimes do this	We often do this	We do this consistently
Individual					
Individuals are recognized and rewarded for their sales teamwork.					
Support people consider themselves to be part of the sales team.					
Opportunity Management					
We map our organizational chart to that of the buyer's so that team members know their assigned stakeholders.					
Before every major investment of time and resource in an account, strategy review sessions are held.					

Best Practice, Teamwork	Importance	Execution			
	Degree of Importance (1 = low 10 = high)	Agree, but we never do this	We sometimes do this	We often do this	We do this consistently
Account Management					
Each account has a clear owner to which team members are accountable.					
Split credits are settled up-front and support our strategy.					
We have global account coverage with well-defined roles for all members.					
Industry/Marketplace					
We have a strong sales culture. Selling skills are recognized, rewarded, and reinforced in our company.					

SECTION V

TECHNOLOGY

TECHNOLOGY

It has become appallingly obvious that our technology has exceeded our humanity.

Albert Einstein

CRM—RELATIONSHIPS, WHERE ART THOU?

While there have been some successes, customer relationship management (CRM), as it has been executed, has become one of the biggest misnomers in the business world.

It hasn't been about customers, it hasn't been about relationships, and it hasn't been about management. In fact, when done poorly, CRM can serve as a *barrier* between you and your best clients. In reality, CRM has been about cost reduction, and the net effect has been to commoditize relationships by allowing customers to have a "personal" relationship *with a computer.*

In my personal life, I have fired four vendors who implemented CRM systems badly: my landscape chemical company, a florist, my home alarm company, and several banks. (In fact, I was bank-free for over 15 years. I moved everything to an online brokerage account.)

My landscape chemical company was the first to go. I have been blessed to own 12 acres, just north of Atlanta. Although I have a large yard, I represented only one account to this particular company. Different zones in my yard require different care, and because the company didn't have mapping capabilities, its system had only one description for my yard. On top of that, every time they changed drivers, we had to start all over because their system did not provide continuity of information, which is one of the primary purposes of a CRM system.

The next to go was my florist. Several years ago we had a personal tragedy in our family and I needed five flower arrangements on a Friday, the beginning of a holiday weekend, for a funeral on Saturday. I called my usual florist and explained the situation. I told the salesperson that I would be right over (the store was only a few blocks away). When I got there, the store was closed. I got on my cell phone again and called the salesperson back.

"I am standing outside your door, and it doesn't look like anyone is inside," I said.

There was a long pause.

"Can I please speak to a manager?" I asked.

Another long pause.

"Where are you?" I demanded.

"In Denver," she said.

When I asked her why she didn't tell me this when I first called, she explained that the shop had recently been acquired by a larger company, and all the records had been moved over to a new system.

I canceled my order and called a local florist, Nature's Rainbow, who already had my preferences and credit card on file. The salesperson told me that he would have five flower arrangements ready the next day, and that he would work as long as it took to get them done. Guess who had my business from then on?

My home alarm company was next. A few years ago, my house was struck by lightning, and it knocked out my alarm system. I called the 800 number to ask the company for help. The person on the other end was polite enough, but I soon realized that she was in Salt Lake City. My records, she told me, were in Kansas City—again because of a merger, which happens often in this industry.

I was incredulous. This was the number my wife was supposed to call if there was a burglary attempt while I was out of town! Now I deal with a local company, and my representative is good ole' Alan. The last time I called him with a problem, he said, "Oh, yeah—that's the switch over by the window. It's always been a problem. I'll stop by on my way home tonight."

Give me high touch over high tech.

Bankers. Where do I start? I have a credit card from a bank that is now one of the largest in the United States. They were nice enough to give it to me when I graduated from college and had *no* money (this is either a great investment in me or terrible credit checking, but I'm glad to have the card). I've kept it for 32 years. Today, when I put that card into an ATM machine, the very first question the machine asks me is what language I speak. Thirty-two years and they don't even know which language I speak? How is that for customer intimacy?

When I go in and speak to a teller face-to-face, the first thing he asks me is if I have photo identification. For 20 years in Atlanta I couldn't get a banker to learn my name. I was running a large region for a major software company where we had a new hire almost every other week. I could have brought in a lot of nice accounts. But not once did I ever have a branch banker come out of his cave in the back to learn my name.

Much less, not one of those bankers—until this year— learned my business and provided advice on how to run it. Finally, I found a banker I like: Jim Pope of Ironstone Bank. He knows me, has invited me to play golf, and checks on me to ask about my business and my needs. I actually walked into the bank building a few weeks ago and was greeted across the lobby by Caren Lightfoot from behind the teller window. I asked to see one of the executives, but when she learned what my issue was (a deposit and a check written at the same time), she handled it herself. She said, "I know your relationship with the bank and what other funds you have. We'll be fine." I never thought it would happen in my lifetime. Access to information made it possible, but a caring person made it happen.

When I need something or know that someone is looking for a good banker, I have somebody to call. This is why small banks are booming. When it comes to relationships, they are actually doing what the big banks *say* they do in their ads.

My insurance agent is next. He thinks a relationship is sending calendars and refrigerator magnets once a year.

CRM: COST-REDUCTION MANAGEMENT

The reason many CRM systems have been implemented poorly is that their objective has been a lie. It was never about customers or relationships in the first place.

The true objective when it comes to many of these systems is lowering costs. The idea is that if you can move a customer to a call center from a sales call, your cost drops from $200 to around $25. Even better, if you can move the customer out of the call center and onto the Web, it drops to about 17 cents. Lowering costs in this age of the "China effect"—the epidemic of cost containment—means that in some cases companies have become more efficient at providing Internet or call-center service for very low margin accounts.

But the disease has spread over to large-margin relationships where companies are treating their best business customers like commodities, making them wait in long hold lines. "Please wait while our agents are servicing other customers" often means "We haven't hired enough people to take care of our clients, so you have to wait."

The next objective of the CRM system has been to get the "little black book" out of the heads of

> "Please wait while our agents are servicing other customers" often means "We haven't hired enough people to take care of our clients, so you have to wait."

salespeople and into the computer so that, if and when the salespeople leave, they don't take their names and contacts with them. In reality, if they have built relationships with these contacts, they still take the relationships with them.

Whenever you have turnover in your sales force—on your side or on the client's side—emotional bank accounts, as referred to by Stephen Covey in his book, *The Seven Habits of Highly Effective People*, go back to zero.

The real issue is turnover. If companies spent a fraction of the money solving their sales turnover problem that they do trying to automate their sales force to solve customer problems, they might start to build some real relationships.

But getting all the information and contacts into the computer is designed so that no one person *has* to have a relationship with the client. We can swap people out as the call centers change shifts. In direct field sales and marketing, though, capturing the little black book and ignoring the turnover problem simply won't work.

While it is true that information is important to relationships, it is only a tool. There are missing links between our objective in the account—account dominance or preferred vendor status—and an information tool (see Figure 7–1).

Let's work backwards: If you want to dominate an account, what the client wants is *trust*. Trust is built over time. Relationships are built over time. In complex sales, people buy from people—not computers. You *can* sell online, but not if you want trust. Not if you want account dominance.

FIGURE 7-1 The missing links between CRM and a relationship.

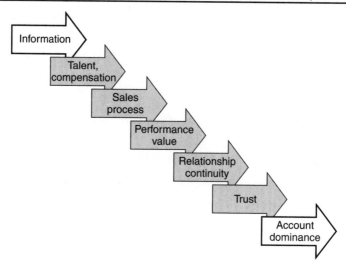

If you want to sell commodities, sell them over the Web and service them with a call center—the same for noncompetitive reorders. But strategic business-to-business (B2B) services and products include greater career risk to the buyer and therefore require trust. In order to maintain trust, you need *continuity of the relationship*, yet sales turnover in the high-tech industry averages around 30 percent per year.

A CRM system is a repository for information—not a process. Information about problem resolution and purchasing history is very important, but only to the degree that it builds trust and continuity so that clients don't have to constantly train new salespeople on how to sell to them. In addition to this continuity, the company has to have delivered value because performance on the last sale is the gateway to repeat business. When your product or solution is performing and producing results and value—and you have documented those results—then risk begins to lower.

As risk lowers, trust goes up. This is why IBM was able to sell its products for such a premium in the 1980s. The company lowered risk for IT directors. In order to do this, you have to have a sales process that rewards not just customer satisfaction but also customer loyalty. And there is a big gap between the two.

A CRM system is a repository for information, not a process.

In some studies, there is as much as a 40 percent gap between customer satisfaction and customer loyalty. Satis-

Several years ago, Blake Batley met with a vice president of sales of a large CRM software provider and asked him, "What makes your CRM application so much better than all the other CRM applications in the market that seem to be positioned the same way?"

The vice president said, "Well, our application is great because it gives our clients insight into all the history and interactions they have had with their own customers."

"But how does your CRM application help your salespeople defeat your competition?" Blake asked. "How does it help them win deals and make their numbers?"

The vice president didn't have an answer.

Having access to contacts and a customer history alone doesn't help you win deals.

fied customers will still buy from somebody else. As Herb Cohen, the great negotiating trainer, said in one of his speeches, "They care, but not that much."

Technology can't make up for what hit-and-run selling does to destroy trust. And if you want to be trusted, you have to have trustworthy people—people who can sell consultatively, who know their clients' business as well as they do their own, and who are willing to work collaboratively to solve business problems.

David Stargel, our principal in charge of the Deloitte account, relates this story. A partner at Deloitte called on an executive client, and although the executive didn't have any work for the consultant, he agreed to meet with him anyway.

A few months later, the partner called on the executive again. He still didn't have any work for him, but again, they met anyway.

The executive continued to meet with the consultant every time he called on him, never having any work for his firm, for 15 months. Finally, at the end of those 15 months, the executive called the consultant with a project.

The consultant excitedly offered to get his team together and present a proposal.

"That won't be necessary," the executive told him. "The last 15 months have been a test. If you will stay with me when I am not buying anything, I am confident you will stay with me when I am."

Information is vital to the degree that it supports all these missing links and strategies. As Klaus Besier, who grew SAP America in its early days, says, "Knowledge of birthdays alone is not going to give you competitive advantage."

If your objective is to reduce cost and you end up nickel-and-diming your clients by not giving them adequate service, then a bad CRM implementation can ultimately cost you.

FIELD SALES FORCES SERVED LAST

Many CRM initiatives are ill fated when they get to the field sales force because they are implemented by IT and implemented backwards. Considering the system first—and then addressing the needs of marketing, legal, and customer service—before *finally* talking to your sales force about their sales process and what they need to improve, is the wrong approach.

The result is asking your primary revenue generators to do data entry for the rest of the firm. Think about the basic economics of this: If a salesperson has a yearly quota of $2 million and works 2,000 hours in a year, he or she must sell $1,000/hour to make quota. Yet the CRM implementation wants you to make that salesperson into a $1,000/hour data-entry clerk—for the benefit of everyone else (see Figure 7–2).

A better approach, seconded by Joe Galvin of Gartner, Inc., is to start with a sales process. First, identify your best practices sales process, all the way from demand cre-

FIGURE 7–2   Get your process straight—then automate.

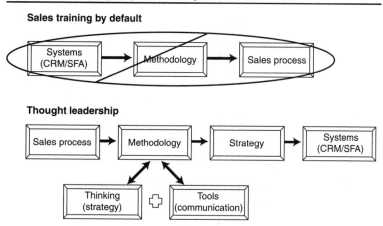

ation through competition to contract and then to account control.

"Gartner Dataquest has recognized that enterprises have spent more than $3.6 billion on sales software alone, with growth projected through 2007," says Galvin. "However, many of these investments have failed to deliver measurable results, characterized by extremely low adoption rates or total abandonment."

Galvin further states that, "sales culture dictates, to a large degree, technology adoption," and "technology alone will not change behavior."[1]

Defining your best practice sales cycle with your management team is the starting point for almost all things in sales effectiveness. Out of this exercise, you can identify—in each phase—what questions should be asked, what actions should be taken, and who is responsible.

[1] Joe Galvin, *Technology-Powered Sales Productivity* (Gartner, Inc. 2004), pp. 6–10.

Take that sales process and combine it with a methodology that incorporates tactics, the impact of time, the hierarchy of pain, political navigation, and consultative selling, and out of this comes a strategy that will drive your sales activity. This becomes the "playbook" for your team.

Most information systems are used simply to provide access to your process, to document your chosen strategy to the rest of the sales team, and to give managers a tool from which to coach.

This is not about filling out forms or screens. It's about how you *think* and how you *lead*.

There are two purposes to creating a sales plan. The first is to stimulate thinking and make sure that you haven't forgotten things. Pilots, whether they have been flying for 3 months or 30 years, still use a checklist.

This is not about filling out forms or screens. It's about how you *think* and how you *lead*.

The second purpose of a sales plan is to communicate your strategy to your manager, who may be able to help you with your strategy, and to your teammates, who need to know who is responsible for which actions, which messages, which stakeholders, and when each activity is due.

This is a major area in which salespeople must move from loners to leaders. Lots of salespeople like to keep this in their head, and as a result, the forecast suffers, the presentations suffer because teammates don't know what is expected of them, and prospects suffer because they have to sit through endless presentations that don't address their pains.

"Meeting demands for increased visibility does not help salespeople or organizations sell more," Galvin says. "The reporting of pipeline and forecast values to meet requirements of CEOs and CFOs has little impact on individual or organizational productivity. To increase productivity, sales executives should focus the execution of the sales methodology and processes that accelerate selling, not the reporting requirement of finance."

It's about communication, your plan, and leading your team. Your process needs to drive your technology, not vice versa.

TOOLS FOR THE INDIVIDUAL SALESPERSON

It is helpful to examine technology in light of how it empowers the four levels of sales strategy. At the bottom are tools that empower selling to individuals, or face-to-face selling. Obviously, these are the contact and activity managers, and there are many vendors in this area. This has been one of the most productive areas for information technology in assisting salespeople.

Not only has new technology given salespeople a tool for searching and finding contacts earlier and then generating e-mails and correspondence more quickly, but it also gets the information, which is a company asset, out of the salesperson's head and into the corporate system.

A well-known fact among salespeople, however, is that almost every salesperson has two databases: one that is shared with the company and one that they keep in Outlook or ACT or some other database of contacts that doesn't really belong to the company. This is only natural, but it still means that every time a salesperson has to enter a contact, it may have to be entered in two places.

Network Management Tools

Some of the more innovative technology tools in the area of contact management for selling at the individual level (as of the date of this book) are those offered by such companies as Spoke, LinkedIn, and Plaxo that allow you to electronically validate your contact information, keep up with changes, and find out where people in your network have moved.

Spoke and LinkedIn have an interesting approach in that they acknowledge that the key to political navigation is sponsorship. They allow you to link people into your network—and vice versa—so that you can find out who actually knows whom. In this way, if you can't get access to someone, you can get sponsorship from someone else who has access to that person. This kind of political navigation is one of the most effective ways of gaining access to executives. You can borrow influence from someone you know to get to someone you don't.

These companies have moved beyond contact management to linking networks and saving salespeople dozens and dozens of phone calls to find out who in their firm or industry knows someone who can help them get that precious first 30 minutes of access.

TECHNOLOGY-ASSISTED OPPORTUNITY COACHING

A contact manager is not adequate for opportunity management, and neither is the simple forecast that comes with most CRM systems. Among the best practices we see in opportunity management tools are:

- A lead prequalification checklist

- A prospect qualification checklist

- A competitive assessment

- A value linkage chart

- A stakeholder analysis

- An action plan

- Coaching questions

Lead Prequalification Checklist

Marketing tends to measure its success by the quantity of leads generated by any given campaign. But the sales department is frustrated when it receives a blizzard of unqualified "leads" from marketing, most of which will not turn into prospects even after hours of phone calls.

Research shows that a very large number of these leads are never followed up on at all, probably because of the low-quality experience of previous leads.

Jim Ninivaggi, director of the sales performance practice at SiriusDecisions, a sales effectiveness analyst firm, says:

In some organizations, up to 90 percent of leads don't get followed up on at all. If I get 100 leads and only two pan out, the next time I get 100 leads, I'll ignore them because they aren't worth my time.

Of these leads that aren't getting followed up on, most of those prospects will buy something in the next 12 to 18 months. They may not buy it from you, but the interest level was usually high enough that they will probably buy something.

It is more economic to have a marketing person nurture these leads than to have a field person follow them up. This is where marketing can play a very effective role.

Prospect Qualification Checklist

An agreed-on set of qualification criteria not only prompts the salesperson to identify the risks of proceeding but also removes the emotional issue of qualifying out versus quitting. In this way, you have the proper expectations for the forecast because everyone is using the same standards.

What are our agreed-on criteria for pursuing this opportunity? Will they buy from anybody? Will they buy from us? How does this prospect compare with our other opportunities? Do we have the resources?

Competitive Assessment

The key to competitive tactics is timing and anticipation. A technology that prompts our thinking promotes earlier action and competitive advantage.

How do we compare against our competitor in this account? Do we have a good chance to win? What are our relative strengths and weaknesses compared with their needs? Do we have any unique differentiators? What strategies can we anticipate from each competitor? How do we beat them out of the starting blocks?

Value Linkage Chart

A tool that helps us think through our value proposition allows us to present and focus benefits and messages to the right stakeholders without them having to figure it all out by themselves (and sometimes get it wrong). How do our solutions link into their issues and needs? Who cares? Does our value proposition link into strategic initiatives or issues? What cultural, financial, political, and strategic benefits can we offer?

Stakeholder Analysis

Who will be involved in the evaluation? Who matters? What part will they play? What is their current preference? How much power and influence do they have? How do we win their vote? How can we live without their vote?

Action Plan

This is the outcome of the analysis and strategy review. It is the purpose of a sales process. Without it, people wander in an account, waiting for things to happen. The most important impact of technology in this area is the ability to adjust the plan purposefully and dynamically through online strategy conferences with teammates who may be remote.

What actions are needed to win this opportunity? Who is the owner of each action item? When is it due? How will each competitor respond?

Coaching Questions

While there is no substitute for a manager's coaching to challenge assumptions and blind spots, embedding the list of questions to ask the customer and yourself about your strategy is a useful tool to jog salespeople's minds about all the issues they need to cover. This "coach in a box," in an automated opportunity management system, not only reminds reps of the training concepts back in the binder in their office but also eliminates "ambush coaching" because all the questions have been previously defined. The result is competitive information earlier and fewer blind spots later.

A Picture Is Worth a Thousand Sales

One of the most useful technology tools we have seen is color-coded organizational charts of the stakeholder analysis. These charts are generated automatically from the opportunity management tool that we use with our clients, and they help sales managers to immediately visualize who in the organization prefers us and how much power they have.

Most veteran managers can take one look at this and drill down to about a dozen questions that not only will purify the forecast but also will help to bring a value-added coaching session to the salesperson to improve his or her strategy.

STOP FLOGGING THE FORECAST—START COACHING TO WIN

Too often, most sales coaching consists of little more than the basic questions of "how much and when" and brings no value to the salesperson whatsoever. In discovery for a recent speech in Europe, the sales executive of a Fortune 500 company admitted, "We are a very process-oriented company, but we are under such quarterly pressure that our account reviews focus too much on *when* we are going to get business and *how much* rather than *what we're going to do* to win it."

There are questions that the sales rep asks the client. There are questions that the reps should ask themselves. And then there are questions that a coach should ask the rep. There are over 100 in all that we have documented from some of the best salespeople in the world. This is how many it takes to win a complex sale.

Traditional questions asked of salespeople by sales managers typically include, for example: What are your differentiators that will cause them to buy from you? What is the source of urgency that will cause them to buy *now*? How will they make the decision? Whose votes really matter on the committee? Why would they buy from you? Do enough important decision makers prefer you to win? Who cares about your benefits, differentiators, and value?

This checklist can be automated as part of a drill-down forecast so that the vice president of sales can see the manager's confidence level in the sales plan and the chances of winning.

This practice is spotty at best in most organizations and missing altogether in many others. Look for these organizations in the financial section of the newspaper when they miss next quarter's earnings.

Coaching in Eight Simple Questions

Exactly what the 100 questions are needs to be validated by your sales managers for your industry and solution set. It is one of the first things we do with a client. But many managers have found it helpful to categorize them into eight universal questions that everyone can keep in their head or on a wallet card:

1. Why buy?	Pains, gains, needs, value, fit, budget
2. Why us?	Differentiation, prior preference
3. Why now?	Source of urgency
4. How much?	Proposed solution, amount, approval process
5. Why them?	Qualification
6. Who matters?	Politics, roles, decision-making process
7. Who cares?	Linkage, preference
8. What next?	Strategy, action items, due date, owner
Copyright © 2005, The Complex Sale, Inc.	

The top salespeople we know discover 80 percent or more of the information they need early in the sales cycle and either qualify out or pursue. Mediocre salespeople usually have less than 50 percent of the information late in the game. Coaches help the average salesperson to fill in blind spots and challenge assumptions earlier to gain advantage.

A good coaching session not only can improve the chance of winning, but also improve the forecast as well. The coaching process lies above the sales process and is an "analysis of the analysis" from a more experienced eye.

Our principal, Phil Johnson, has worked with several of our clients to include the front-line sales managers' analysis and confidence rating in the salesperson's plan as part of the official forecasting system.

A major flaw in current forecasting philosophy is to multiply the percentage of your chances to win by the value of the deal to get an expected value for the opportunity. This is usually reduced by the manager based on his or her confidence in the rep rather than the analysis. All of the opportunities on the forecast are then combined in the hope that the law of large numbers will get us to a total figure that is somewhere close. *In reality, deals are binary. You either lose them or win them.*

Phil's approach of including a confidence rating feedback system from strategy reviews ensures not only that the analysis is being conducted on a periodic basis but also that the forecast reflects the realities of winning rather than a probable expected value for each deal. This is a new way of thinking about a forecast.

There is a symbiotic relationship between good coaching questions and the activities in a best practice sales cycle. The coaching questions are what the salesperson needs to *know* in order to win the deal. The activities are the things the salesperson needs to *do* to find out what he or she needs to *know*.

Answering the questions isn't about filling out a form— *it's getting the information it takes to win.* If your sales management team doesn't have the *discipline* to require salespeople to get this information and get it early, then your organization doesn't have the discipline to win, no matter what technology you use.

Too often coaching is really a "review" of where you are and have been in an account or opportunity. True coaching is discussing blind spots, strategy, and actions to support both accounts and opportunities. A good coach can help a salesperson challenge what he or she doesn't know or is assuming and then build actions to fill the gaps. A key value that coaches bring to sales reps is to anticipate competitive responses and prepare counterstrategies. Better information leads to a better strategy.

PIPELINE VERSUS FORECAST

Unfortunately, a large number of deals that are on the forecast have already spun out of control owing to one event or another. Consequently, every pipeline also should include "suspects" so that sales managers can start asking pointed questions and coaching salespeople how to get in control of these deals early in the cycle. *This is the difference between a forecast and a pipeline.* And this is also where a good CRM system allows sales managers to track lead quality and responsiveness.

Forecast or "Pastcast"—Driving in the Rearview Mirror

Many sales managers don't review or coach forecast and pipeline opportunities early enough to make a difference because of the current quarterly focus. Public companies' deals generally don't get reviewed until the quarter in which they are forecasted to close. If the average sales cycle at a company is six months, the deal is not being focused on until it is in its last 90 days.

Think about how big of an issue this is if the sales cycle is 12 months. This would mean that the deal was ignored by management for nine months! This is aggravated by salespeople who don't want the manager's scrutiny on the deal until it is either virtually closed or in trouble.

Every manager should schedule coaching sessions for all pipeline deals, no matter how far out they are. These sessions should occur once during the early part of a quarter, when you can focus more on the long term, and then again when the deal is moving to the next phase of the sales cycle. Or the sessions should happen before each major phase of the sales cycle that requires additional resources (see Figure 7–3).

FIGURE 7–3   Three-dimensional (3-D) drill-down forecasting system.

Sales Forecast					
Account	Opportunity	Rep Name	$Amount	Due Date	Sales Phase
xxxxx	xxxxx	xxxxx	xxxxxx.xx	xx/xx/xx	xxxx
xxxxx	xxxxx	xxxxx	xxxxxx.xx	xx/xx/xx	xxxx
xxxxx	xxxxx	xxxxx	xxxxxx.xx	xx/xx/xx	xxxx
xxxxx	xxxxx	xxxxx			
xxxxx	xxxxx	xxxx			

Sales Manager's Strategy Review Confidence Rating	High	Med	Low
Why buy?—Value proposition?	x		
Who matters?—Access to power?			
Why us?—Preference for us?	x		
Why them?—Qualified prospect?			
Why now?—Source of urgency?			
What next?—Strategy & actions?	x		

Sales Rep Opportunity Plan
Value proposition, solution linkage to pain
Stakeholder analysis, preference, org. chart
Strategic plan & action items
Qualification criteria
Decision-making process, politics
Competitive analysis & counterstrategy

COMPETITIVE INTELLIGENCE TECHNOLOGIES

In addition to a sales planning and communication tool, several other technologies enable effective opportunity management. In the area of competitive intelligence, as part of your knowledge management strategy, it is important to have a repository and a dedicated resource committed to gathering information about specific competitors to equip the field sales force with tactics to respond to competitive traps, objections, messages, and strategies.

One of the first things we do with our clients is work on their competitive sales messaging in four areas: what we say about the competition, what we say about us, what they say about us, and what they say about them. Of course, this is done in a professional manner, but if you know your competitors, you can defeat them at three levels: at the company-to-company level, at the product or solution level, and at the person-to-person level (see Figure 7–4).

Competitive interactions occur every day, but are you learning from them? Some historians say that the Allies in World War II were able to win because, even though they were unprepared, they were able to learn faster from their defeats and failures and more quickly develop new tactics and weapons.

What strategies are the competition using? How have they beaten you recently? When and how did you beat them? What differentiators and tactics are they using?

FIGURE 7–4 Competitive messaging.

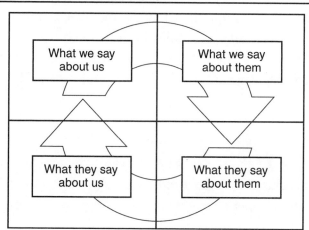

Gathering this information should not be a haphazard effort. Depending on the size of your company, you may choose to have this done in marketing, or you can out-source it.

Many companies outsource this to firms such as Primary Intelligence, a company with which we partner. Primary Intelligence and firms like it research competitors for their clients, uncovering their strengths and weaknesses and anticipating how they are going to compete against them.

There are also new technologies from companies such as Involve Technology that allow you to glean information from your own people and distribute it in a more efficient manner than many-to-many e-mails.

Involve Technology has a new enabling tool (at the

point of this writing) that allows each salesperson in the field to input competitive tactics, messages, traps, objections, and so on on a daily basis, where they are then "scrubbed" by somebody in product marketing for duplication and legal issues and made available instantly to the

Air Force Colonel John Boyd discovered that the speed of information drives the speed of strategy, which then drives competitive advantage. His theories of maneuver warfare, based on competitive intelligence, revolutionized our military between Vietnam and the Gulf War.

Boyd led the design of the F-15, F-16, and A-10 fighter planes. He was the first graduate of the Air Force fighter weapons school to become an instructor immediately upon graduation. He was called "40-Second Boyd" because he would bet anyone that they could start on his tail and he could shoot them down within 40 seconds. He never had to pay.

He proved that the F-86 had a 10:1 kill ratio in Korea against the MIG (which was an equal airplane) simply because it had a bubble canopy. Our pilots were able to see the enemy first and anticipate their tactics. About 80 percent of the time, the pilot who sees first wins.

The principles contained in Boyd's books, and in those about him, have much to say about business and sales strategy as well as resistance to changing cultures.

rest of the company. The key is that this system is driven by a content-sensitive search engine that allows salespeople to find the information they need quickly and efficiently.

Salespeople should have access to what the competition is planning to do because, in competitive positioning, the advantage lies in saying it first. If you know that a competitor is going to raise an issue, it's better that you raise it first. If possible, neutralize it and position it as an advantage for you.

> In competitive positioning, the advantage lies in saying it first.

If your competitor is allowed to come in and say things unchallenged or unanticipated, he or she gains an incredible amount of power. It takes up to 10 times more resources and effort to change someone's mind than it does to help make it up in the first place. You can see why timely knowledge management can have a significant impact on competitive advantage.

If you plan to compete in a professional manner, you must anticipate issues and shape them—often without mentioning your competitor by name. Instead, you can say, "Other firms approach this area in this way. Here is our approach, and this is why we think it is superior." The chances of having this perceived positively are much greater if you can anticipate the competition's move.

TOOLS FOR ACCOUNT MANAGEMENT

In the area of account management, the technology bar is raised once again. Not only do we need to manage an opportunity and the politics and pains therein, but if we're trying to dominate a global account or we have a major strategic account, we also need to know the current status of every opportunity. If we don't, the results can be disastrous.

This is where a CRM system can be of great value in identifying and cataloging opportunities worldwide.

Jon Hauck was delivering a Total Enterprise Account Management (T.E.A.M.) workshop to the Daimler Chrysler account team of one of our clients with attendees from the United States, Germany, and several other countries. The goal of the workshop was to build a global account plan.

As they went through the process, they discovered that the prospect actually had *four* strategic business units involved in the decision-making process, not three as they had originally thought!

This led to a call to the CIO, which resulted in identifying a key pain around a quality initiative, all unknown to the account team. Based on this knowledge, they were able to develop a plan to compete for, and ultimately win, the business.

Had they not invested in the account planning process and gotten everyone to collaborate on a plan, they would have missed a huge opportunity from a division that they didn't even know existed.

With greater visibility into all opportunities throughout the world, by having all opportunities on the same system, you can achieve greater access, avoid conflicting pricing, and structure joint proposals that the competition can't match. At the account management level, you also need to be able to drill down into individual opportunities to find out if they can be combined with other opportunities to outflank the competition. *In many cases you have a better chance of winning a bigger deal than winning a smaller one.*

NEW RESEARCH TOOLS

One of the first things we need to do is research the account and be very knowledgeable about the strategic issues and initiatives so that we can talk intelligently with executives, link our solutions to their high-level initiatives, and earn greater than commodity pricing. Technology and the Internet have been invaluable in enabling companies such as Hoovers and OneSource to gather information from a wide variety of sources and put it all in one place so that salespeople can quickly get the names of the executives, the issues, and the background information they need before calling on an account.

But outside electronic research is not enough. What you need to identify is *pain, initiatives,* and *issues.* The best source of this can be reporters and financial analysts. These people are paid to dig in and find the big, snarling, nasty problems that executives are embarrassed to admit.

Benchmarks for Pain Creation

Another good research organization for finding pains and issues for demand-creation selling is a company called Stratascope, Inc. Stratascope gathers industry statistics and available data on companies based on their financial reports. The company then works with salespeople to help them identify areas where an organization has a gap between its statistics or financial ratios and the industry standard. Using information from Stratascope, if an organization has a solution to the problem, they can actually create a value proposition based on closing that gap.

For example, a prospect averages 83 days sales outstanding in accounts receivable. The industry standard is 67, and the best in industry is 59. Based on the prospect's financials, if you (the salesperson) can close that gap to meet the industry standard, you can show the prospect the savings and return on investment (ROI) he or she would experience as a result of implementing your solution. Maybe the result is an increase in earnings, more freed-up cash, or even an increase in shareholder value by a penny a share. This is a powerful approach in demand-creation selling that the consultants have been using for years.

OBSTACLES TO EFFECTIVE ACCOUNT MANAGEMENT

There are some major organizational and cultural barriers to effective account management that are above and beyond what technology can solve. One is split policy and revenue recognition. Another is turf guarding, and a third, obviously, is communication.

Some salespeople would rather have 100 percent of zero than give up a percentage to someone else. This is the "me" mentality, and this mind-set has to be defeated internally in your culture if you are going to have a successful account management program.

Two of the bigger barriers to technology at the account management level are personal compensation issues and regional boundaries. When SAP was very small, it dominated several accounts because one salesperson could handle a major global account. When SAP became entrenched in other countries, there were internal fights in these accounts over whose share was whose.

The challenge is to keep these struggles internal and away from the client. Never let your service levels be affected by internal arguments.

The people who are probably the best, but not perfect, at this are actually the big consulting houses. For one, they have good revenue recognition—split policies that recognize who sold it and who has to support it. They also evaluate each other in regard to promotions and advancement in making partner. They know that they are going to need another partner some day down the road on their own deal, so, for the most part, collaboration is part of their culture.

They are usually able to put the good of the client above their internal priorities in order to make the pie bigger. Not that there are not fights, but they seem to have a collaborative approach—more so than many of the product companies we work with.

In addition to listing research and opportunities, one of the key places where technology can be of help is to create a balance sheet of political assets—a metric of relationships— within a company. This is a way of measuring preference for you and your firm with powerful executives between the sales.

Building preference must be done before a formal buying event takes place because then the lights come on, the guards go out, and the walls come down.

If you have a good account plan and the technology to make it available to everyone with a need to know, you can set clear goals and leverage your team. Everyone who touches the account in the organization knows what the objective is and can use the normal give and take of daily business to trade for access to the people you need to meet. Without a written companywide plan, and a system to make it accessible, this is simply not going to happen. There is also no way to present your documented value and negotiate it for preferred-vendor status.

Keeping track of multiple divisions and multiple sales efforts—while making sure that your pricing isn't all over the board and providing a convincing joint proposal for the client that will help him or her understand your advantages—takes a great deal of coordination. Solving the political problems inside may be the biggest challenge. Without a piece of technology to keep track of who is doing what, however, this becomes an even more difficult task.

CLOSING THE GAP BETWEEN MARKETING AND SALES

Another important area of automation—that of sales messaging—can greatly affect the interface between marketing and sales. This is an area where technology actually has exacerbated the problem.

Marketing serves many important functions. Among these is creating effective and timely sales messaging for salespeople. Often the sales department is unable to get the information it needs from marketing in a format its people can use.

With the advent of e-mail and the Web, marketing people now can barrage salespeople with tons and tons of information, which makes sorting through it all to find the right information even more difficult.

The key to this is to provide the information in a format that allows salespeople to find what they need quickly and easily. Another problem is that marketing typically doesn't create different messages for prospects, customers, salespeople, and investors. And if a company has a large number of products, a large number of competitors, and is in a number of different industries, the result is a huge knowledge management problem—which drives a sales problem.

Hey, Marketing—Salespeople Are Your Customers, Too

Marketing collateral and brochures obviously should be written from the point of view of the customer. But which customer? For sales-effectiveness messages, the starting point should be from the salesperson's point of view, which is by stakeholder. What do the salespeople need to be competitive, to keep customers satisfied, to add value, and to win more business?

Once you have this information, it has to be organized and indexed. First, it has to be chunked into pieces. Some companies approach this by chunking it by product, *but salespeople need it by customer pain—from the customer's point of view*. If customers have this pain, how does our solution solve it? What are the outcomes? And—oh, by the way—it is contained in what product?

After the information has been segmented, it then has to be indexed so that salespeople can search for it by customer pain; by product, solution, or service; by industry, executive, and technical buyer; by phase of the sales cycle; and by competitor. Once indexed, it must be linked to other

You are a salesperson in a hotel room, late at night. Tomorrow morning, you have a sales call to a CFO in health care, against competitor XYZ, for a certain solution set. What do you say? What are the industry issues for each person on the buying committee? What will your competitor have said? What traps can you look for? What issues can you create?

Tomorrow afternoon, you have to talk to procurement in Bank X. What are their issues? What will they be concerned about? What solutions do you have? How can you differentiate yourself?

relevant data so that salespeople can trace it back to other related information that they might need.

As you can see, this can be a knowledge management challenge. Most file document vendors organize and index documents, but salespeople need their information in a more granular fashion.

Sales Knowledge Management

Salespeople tell us that they often have to make as many as 20 calls internally to find the information they need for prospects and clients. A tool that makes this easier is an enormous value that frees salespeople up to sell.

An example of a vendor working to provide that additional level of value to salespeople is Pragmatech. The company's offerings allow salespeople to quickly personalize communication in the context of "buyer-ready information." In other words, the communication is personalized and tailored to the buying criteria of each prospect or customer. All Pragmatech applications are driven by a common knowledge base. Content in the knowledge base is parsed into customizable pieces and indexed with appropriate search engines so that salespeople can easily personalize presentations, proposals, statements of work, RFP responses, business letters, and other communications throughout the sales process.

Jennifer Webb of Pragmatech tells us that when the company surveys its clients, it finds that 90 percent of the sales messaging used by its salespeople comes from their own hard drives—not a central message center—and that much of the data is feature-driven rather than pain-driven. When Pragmatech talks to prospects, its people ask, "What if you could capture what your A players are saying and get that into the heads of your B and C players?"

Pragmatech's success stories demonstrate the value of a centralized knowledge base made accessible to sales organizations. For one enterprise, a leading online global career network, the marketing team aligned closely with sales to capture and refine the best high-value buyer-focused messaging. With use of automated proposals and presentations and a searchable Website, the sales force throughout the enterprise had access to these well-articulated and accurate messages and could apply them to communications that were personalized to the buyer's objectives. The results included improvements in sales effectiveness, client interactions, competitive advantages, and productivity.

Salespeople still need the flexibility to tailor messages to individual buyers, but in this way they can at least start from a central repository. Then you can be sure that they are basing their messages on current information that is already arranged into pieces that they can organize and use.

The solution is not just a sales portal, a tool kit, a dashboard, or a marketing encyclopedia. There is no technology "silver bullet" when it comes to sales and CRM.

Messages Focused by Stakeholder

The best practice is to have relevant information, to keep it fresh, and to organize and index it based on what your sales force needs. This should be the point of departure, and it should be driven by the best practices sales cycle, working backwards through marketing to get the right information by industry, stakeholder, organizational chart, solution, product, competitor, customer, prospect, or investor.

The information needs to be segmented, indexed, and linked by a tool that can help salespeople find what they need, when they need it, to win more business. By the time a salesperson gleans all this from brochures or books of binders, well, you can get the idea.

Product Launch or Product Lurch?

And if you are involved in a new product launch, your window of competitive advantage is probably six months before your competitor can bring a new product online. If your salespeople spend half that time creating messages themselves, you've already lost half your opportunity.

A typical scenario for many companies is for marketing to give the salespeople information on a new product or solution in a format that is great for a marketing piece but not great for a competitive sales message to be used throughout the sales cycle.

Each salesperson then "translates" this marketing message into the message he or she needs to support the sales process.

Here is the problem: The "A" players may figure this out quickly and lose *value* for only one or two *weeks*. But it takes the "B" players a little longer, and they may lose one or two *deals* before they figure it out. And how long does it take the "C" players? Somewhere between a long time and never. There is a better way to do this.

The best practice that we have found is that when it comes to competitive information, buyers needs, value propositions, and your benefits and differentiators, these need to be organized in a *context-sensitive search engine rather than in a marketing encyclopedia full of brochures.* The search engine is the key.

A few years ago, Jon Hauck and I met with the company with which we had just been merged.

The manager asked us, "So, what did you guys do about six months ago? All of a sudden, you started turning on a dime. We used to be able to try a new tactic on you half a dozen times before you would finally have a sales meeting and get wise to it. Suddenly you started having an answer ready the very next day. Not only could you handle the objection, but you had set a trap for us and spun it the other way!"

What we had done was use the then-new technology of voice mail to create a clearinghouse of information so that whenever a salesperson discovered something new, he or she passed it through the product and brand managers immediately, and it was back in the field the next day.

The simple use of this technology made millions of dollars for us, but speed was the real issue. Now, with the Internet, this competitive speed should be even easier and faster.

Speed of Feedback Is Advantage

The best practice is to refresh information every 48 hours and to have somebody in charge of each competitor and each industry to keep that information current. You also need a feedback loop where a salesperson in one part of the world who uncovers a competitive trap can spread the word and have the rest of your salespeople ready for it before your competition can use it on you a dozen times.

Technology Scorecard

Best Practices, Technology	Importance	Execution		
	Degree of Importance (1 = low, 10 = high)	Agree, but we never do this	We sometimes do this	We often do this	We do this consistently
Individual				
We have a standard, widely adopted contact management system for our firm.				
Opportunity Level				
We have an effective, widely adopted opportunity management planning tool.				
Our metrics allow sales managers to track lead responsiveness.				
We regularly conduct win–loss reports through a third party.				
Our sales process and methodology are imbedded into our forecasting/pipeline system.				

188

Best Practices, Technology	Importance	Execution			
	Degree of Importance (1 = low, 10 = high)	Agree, but we never do this	We sometimes do this	We often do this	We do this consistently
Our forecast/pipeline system includes early suspects for management visibility.					
Account Management					
Our CRM system gives us visibility into opportunities for a given account worldwide.					
We have a CRM system that is widely adopted by the sales force.					
Industry/Market					
We have a tool for gathering and distributing feedback from our reps quickly.					
Marketing information is organized and indexed by industry, solution set, individual buyer, and competitor.					
Our sales force is equipped with tactics and messages, by industry, to respond to competitive traps and objections.					

SECTION VI

TRUST

CHAPTER

TRUST

I never made a good deal with a bad person, and I never made a bad deal with a good person.

Warren Buffett

Love all, trust a few. Do wrong to none.

William Shakespeare

IT STARTS WITH THE HEART

I've asked many sales managers what they think is the most important thing in selling. Some say that it's closing, some say prospecting, and some say process. I say it's trust.

Trust is always the strategy. Trust isn't about what you do; it's about who you are. If you want to be trusted, you have to be trustworthy first. And it starts with the heart—you can't fake it.

You can lose with a great product and a great company through a weak salesperson whose messages are not be-

I had one salesperson who was struggling in a given year and asked me for advice as his manager. I told him, "I'm your manager and your friend—and you can take it or leave it—but I think I've identified your problem. You are doing almost everything right except one thing: You're a snob. You like the finer things in life—which is fine—but you have no tolerance for those who don't. You basically don't like your customers, and you can't hide it. You aren't a good enough actor—none of us are.

I watched you in one sales call where you were disdainful of the administrative person and barely tolerant of the project leader, and you patronized the decision maker. None of those emotions are genuine. I can see it, and I'm sure they could see it, too. You have to find something about your clients to like and discard the rest. But most of all, you have to be genuine. You have to build sincere relationships that have value."

lieved. All your value can be lost because there is no bridge of trust between the buyer and the seller. All your investment in your company, product, and marketing can be lost just as if it went off the edge of a broken bridge.

Although character is the foundation of trust, most companies don't interview for it, don't require it, and don't reward it. And yet it may be the root cause of most sales turnover, sales losses, and customer problems.

Alignment—Opening the Door to Rapport

The first decision a buyer makes is about the salesperson. The first step in the process is alignment. This is sometimes called *neurolinguistic programming* and means matching one's voice, rate of speech, level of humor, level of familiarity, and body language to those of the buyer. It removes the physical barriers of bias from the salesperson's message.

Alignment is the first step in building rapport. Many salespeople ruin the entire call by aligning badly—becoming too friendly too fast, laughing at things that aren't really funny, being too familiar (this is especially deadly internationally), or dressing inappropriately for that industry.

You can lose a great product and a great company through a weak salesperson whose messages are not believed.

How many salespeople have you met who were too aggressive and turned you off? They could have been selling one dollar bills for 50 cents and you still wouldn't have bought from them. They create barriers to what may be a very sound solution. A good message can be lost through a bad messenger. Sometimes salespeople are so bad at this that they become sales *prevention* people. They just annoy us.

I once walked out of a clothing store that had a suit I had been looking at for months. I ended up leaving because I refused to buy it from that particular salesperson. Unfortunately, when I went back for the suit later, it was gone. I didn't find it again for two years, but it was still better than buying it from that jerk.

I later went to a store where the salesperson knew the manufacturer, called and had them check next year's stock for my material, pull it out of inventory and make my suit. Now I always go there first.

A good message can be lost through a bad messenger.

Alignment can be based on gender, cultural background, or personality. In the movie *My Cousin Vinny*, Joe Pesci plays a New York lawyer who has to try a murder case in a rural Alabama courtroom. When he shows up for court in a leather

The salesperson was ex-IBM and very organized, but he had poor alignment and interpersonal skills. We once went on a sales call to a "good ol' boy" in Alabama. The salesperson began the call by pulling out a checklist of all the things he had done in the sales cycle and started ticking them off one item after another while sitting on the edge of his seat. After listening for a few minutes, the gray-haired IT director leaned back in his chair and said, "Son, you've got a really good memory. Think you can remember your way outta here?" It was over.

This is a case of very bad alignment. Everybody knows that in the South, you spend the first 30 minutes "cracker barreling," talking about traffic, the weather, football, BBQ—*anything* but business. On the other hand, in Manhattan, you have about 30 nanoseconds to get to the point or you must be from somewhere "out West"—like New Jersey. It's called *alignment*. And this salesperson didn't have it.

jacket, the stern, conservative judge eyes him suspiciously and demands angrily, "Mr. Gambini, what are you wearing?" Joe Pesci looks down at his outfit, confused, and says, "Clothes. I don't get the question."

Some people who have become involved with sales don't get the question. Customers have the right to discriminate. And you'll never even know why you lost.

In business, different people align differently with different personalities. Some people like to be approached by task first and then relationship. Others like to establish a relationship before talking about business. Internationally, there are many cultural rites and practices that must be observed. If you get it wrong, your sales call will be ineffective at best—disastrous at worst.

One of our principals, Nick Holbrook, was shopping with his wife for a new car in England, where they live. As they entered the showroom, a salesman appeared and introduced himself to Nick, shaking hands with Nick first and then Sue.

It was the last interaction he had with Sue that afternoon.

Instead, the salesman spent the next 15 minutes asking Nick a series of questions about his budget and timeframe for buying a car. Then he showed the interior and external features of the car to Nick and offered him the keys for a test drive. He asked Nick what he was looking for in an engine, his color preference, and which accessories he would most like to have. Before they left the showroom, he loaded Nick down with brochures about the car, explaining the different makes and models.

But it was *Sue* who was car shopping that day—not Nick. She is also a very successful sales manager for a major software firm. That day, Sue was the decision maker with the sum of all votes plus one.

The salesman lost the sale because he made the false assumption that Nick was driving the decision-making process and held all the power.

As Nick and Sue walked out the front door of the showroom, the salesman made one last-minute effort to reach out to Sue. He called out, "And what about you, Love? I'm sure we could find a nice little run-around for you?"

No understanding, no rapport, no trust, no sale, no going back ever.

Alignment is usually different by industry. Bankers dress and act differently from academics, who dress and act differently from manufacturers. If you are selling to consulting firms—and we learned this early in our company history—you have to do a universal "search and replace" on your vocabulary. Most industries have a language and style of their own, and insiders can spot outsiders easily.

There are a number of training courses to help people with this fundamental skill going all the way back to Meyers-Briggs and DISC—all of which are strong fundamentals and help salespeople match their selling style to the personality of the buyer. The challenge, of course, is to avoid stereotyping by nationality, race, or gender and approach each individual as an individual. Different people want to be sold to in different ways.

One of the most enduring books on this topic is *How to Win Friends and Influence People,* by Dale Carnegie. It has stood the test of time for decades. In his book, Carnegie talks about such tips as learning and saying people's names, the importance of a firm handshake, and finding things in common with other people. As old and fundamental as these concepts are, it is amazing how banks and grocery stores today have never learned the importance of remembering and repeating their customers' names.

Consultative Selling—The Answer Is a Question
Listen, or your tongue will make you deaf.

Cherokee saying

By far the most important step in building rapport is probing and listening. In the early seventies, Neil Rackham, author of the best-seller *SPIN Selling,* was hired by large companies to observe what successful salespeople did right and what unsuccessful salespeople did wrong. Rackham discovered that the best salespeople actually held back the product for the longest time and were not necessarily the best talkers but the best listeners. This was the birth of consultative selling. Listen first, talk second—no matter if it's a one-hour call or an entire-day demo.

And yet, 20 to 30 years later, one of the most common mistakes we find among salespeople is still "dashing to the demo"—running out and showing the product or solution before doing a needs assessment with the client. The reason is this: There is a whole new generation of CEOs, sales managers, and salespeople who have to learn to break this habit all over again.

When I was in the software business and I started doing needs assessments before demos, my partners and I cut our presentations from eight hours to two hours—and they were *better.* The irony was that not only were our presentations more focused, but *we also were winning at the needs assessment— before* the real demo. This is where the selling really took place.

Through better listening and understanding— elbow to elbow with the client, face to face—we not only began to "outcare" the competition, but we also were able to better understand the decision-making process, politics, our competitive position, and the needs of each buyer as an individual, as well as their culture.

By the time we got to the presentation, most of the deals had already been decided (as they are now). We had friends in the audience, we knew their terminology, we knew their strategic issues, and we had planted subtle traps to get the competition reacting to us rather than vice versa.

We began to get inside their competitive loop much earlier, and our presentations were more focused *on their needs* and motivators rather than on our features. In addition, we qualified out of bad deals earlier.

This is especially a problem when selling a complex product or solution. There may be over 100 reasons why someone might buy from you, but they are really only looking for five or so. *Which five?* Or if they're only looking for five or six capabilities of your product and you come

Listen first; talk second—no matter if it's a one-hour call or an entire-day demo.

in talking about 105, not only will you bore them, but you will appear uncaring about their problem. You also will look too complex. This sets you up for commoditization because they see a lot of things in your product that they don't need and don't think they should pay for.

Consultative selling begins to build rapport because you are focused on their issues rather than on your capabilities.

One of our clients tells a story of a sales call early in his career. He sat down with the executive and began to lay out a "partnership" between his organization and the client's. The executive stopped him, midsentence, and retrieved a two-inch stack of business cards from his desk.

"This is a stack of cards from all the different salespeople from all the different divisions of your company who have come to see me in the last two years. I never see the same person twice. When you have called on me for a year and know more about my business than I do, then you can talk to me about being your partner. Until then, you're the vendor and I'm the customer."

After you build rapport, which moves the client to an open state of mind, you can begin building preference.

Growing from rapport to preference to trust takes time. This means that salespeople need to stay on the same accounts long enough to become a source of trust. Every time we churn accounts, we set the registers back to zero. A client relationship management (CRM) system might give you continuity of information, but that's not the same as continuity of a relationship. Trust between people builds over time.

From Rapport to Preference—There Are Two Roads
Building preference is achieved through one of two traditional routes: You either (1) link your solution to your client's pains or gains or (2) build preference through influences and relationships. Preferably, you do both. Most of the earlier selling methodologies address one or the other (see Figure 8–1).

FIGURE 8–1 Pillars of preference.

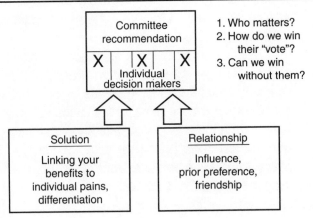

It is important to remember personality types when choosing which of the pillars of trust to build on first. When building preference, not only must you link to solving your client's business problems, but you also have to differentiate why you can do it better—and you need to do it in a *professional* manner.

Competitive selling isn't negative selling unless it's done incorrectly. If you are too heavy-handed too early in your differentiation or too negative, you can come across as defensive and unprofessional. However, if you don't find ways to show why you're better, the client might buy the wrong solution for all the wrong reasons. *You could fail to serve your client by not being aggressive enough.*

> Consultative selling begins to build rapport because you are focused on your client's issues rather than on your capabilities.

How fast you can approach competitive differentiation depends on your relationship with the individual buyer in the particular country or culture that you are in. In the United States, we've had competitive advertising on television for over 20 years. In some countries, however, it's illegal to even mention your competitor. However, there are ways to differentiate yourself without ever mentioning the competitor's name. For example, you can suggest that the client look for a specific capability from all the vendors or ask the same question of everyone including you.

The Differences in Differentiators

Differentiators fall into several categories. There are *unique differentiators*, which are a capability, functionality, or service that you have but that your competitors simply don't offer. Unique differentiators that solve strategic problems for powerful buyers are a salesperson's nirvana. If you ever get in this position, never discount the deal.

Some differentiators are *relative differentiators*. You do it, but so does the competition. In this case, you have to show how you do it faster, better, cheaper, at lower risk, or with more experienced, dependable people than the competition. The consulting industry is full of relative differentiators. There is almost nothing a big consulting firm cannot do with enough time and money. Differentiation there comes from other sources, such as limiting risk, sharing risk, industry focus, qualifications of personnel, or actually meeting and bonding with the people who will be handling your project.

Some differentiators are *motivators,* and others are only *satisfiers.* For a capability to be a motivator, it must present significant political gain, recognition, glory, or lower risk.

I remember hearing one salesperson proclaiming the differentiating advantage of her user groups. Oh, wow. *This* is a compelling value proposition? I don't think anyone ever chose a vendor because he or she had better user groups. This is an example of a *satisfier.* If you didn't have one, it might hurt you, but having one just satisfies an item on a checklist. The higher up the food chain of value toward strategic, financial, political, and cultural

If you don't find ways to show that you're better, the client may buy the wrong solution for all the wrong reasons. *You could fail to serve your client by not being aggressive enough.*

Unique differentiators that solve strategic problems for powerful buyers are a salesperson's nirvana. If you ever get in this position, never discount the deal.

benefits that your solution can provide, the better chance you have of motivating that buyer into action.

Products to Solutions—Want My Trust? Solve My Problem—Want Big Bucks? Solve Big Problems

Alignment and listening are the gateways to rapport. Linking solutions to problems and differentiation begins to build preference. To gain trust, however, you must solve your client's problem. And to move from personal trust to organizational trust, you have to solve bigger, more strategic problems.

"Moving from products to solutions" has been in the sales and marketing vocabulary for over 40 years, but I'm not sure that the average salesperson knows exactly what it means or what his or her contribution is to this process.

It is helpful to start at the origin of the idea. In the early 1980s, Theodore Levitt, in his book, *The Marketing Imagination*, addressed the subject of differentiation beyond the product. Recapping an earlier *Harvard Business Review* article, he wrote of "The Differentiation—of Anything."[1]

His description of the generic product, the expected product, the augmented product, and the potential product defined the conceptual difference between a product and a solution for the next four decades.

Marketing departments seized on the idea early and began expanding offerings and solutions. With the exception of the consulting industry, which has no product to sell, salespeople often have lagged in their ability to sell solutions rather than products (see Figure 8–2).

[1] Theodore Levitt, *The Marketing Imagination* (New York: Free Press, 1983). p. 79.

FIGURE 8-2 Once again, what is a solution?

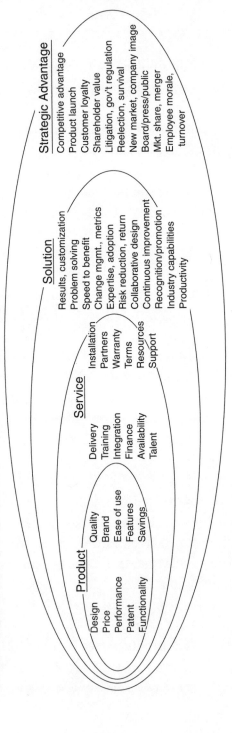

Selling solutions means building trust by lowering risk for the buyer—especially when you deliver results instead of tools. But salespeople have often struggled with *how* they can contribute to the *value* of the solution rather than how they just describe it.

How can salespeople contribute to and be a part of the solution rather than just provide information and entertainment? Salespeople contribute to solution value in the following ways:

- *When they do a better job than the competition of linking the benefits of a complex product to the client's needs.* The more they can link into strategic issues and uniquely differentiate their solution, the more value they can command.

- *When they can help the client to understand the differences between their product and the competitors' and what advantage that brings to the client.*

- *When they can turn relationships into results and lower risk by problem resolution and command of resources within their own company.*

- *When they can understand the political power structure of the buying committee and what part each person will play in the decision-making process.*

- *When they can effectively read accounts, devise and communicate a winning strategy, and lead a sales team to victory.*

- *When they can contribute knowledge to the client beyond their product—industry trends, best practices, in-*

novations, contacts, ideas, benchmarks, and an outside expert's assessment of their own company.

References—A Treasury of Transferred Trust

Because trust is generally low in the early parts of an evaluation, you will need to provide proof statements of your capabilities. This is where references play an active part in your sales process. If you have a capability and your client doesn't, you should encourage thorough reference checking in your client's evaluation process.

References need to be developed and rewarded, and their time needs to be treated respectfully. They deserve notice that they will be called, what the issues may be, and—whereas a reference should not be bought or bribed—they should be rewarded for the time required by extra service, responsiveness, or other acknowledgments.

One caution about giving references before the prospect has "earned" the right to talk to your best customers: Most salespeople don't understand that when you ask a client to be a reference for a particular prospect, you have used up a reference call whether the prospect calls or not. You also have to be careful that you don't give references so early that the prospect calls without enough knowledge to ask the right questions, and your reference is put in the position of being the salesperson.

By the way, calling and debriefing your references after they have been contacted by your prospect is an excellent way to get a perspective on where you are in the sale. The prospect will tell them things that he or she won't tell you. Another way to provide trust in a competitive evaluation is through unsolicited references. If you can get your references to call your prospects and give unsolicited references, that may be even better than simply providing them with a list.

Keep 'Em Honest

Also, never give a list of references to just one person on the buying committee. I've seen an excellent list of references given to somebody on a buying committee and the deal lost to bad references. How does that happen? The person calling probably had negative preference for you and biased the questions or the answers. And since he or she was the only one calling, the result went unchallenged until after the sale.

Give lists to *everyone* on the buying committee. This will keep the checkers honest because they know they aren't the only ones calling. If you think evaluations are conducted fairly and without bias, you can skip this step. But you had better be independently wealthy.

> If you think evaluations are conducted fairly and without bias, you can skip this step. But you had better be independently wealthy.

As preference is built among individuals on the buying team, people start to move beyond neutral to where they really want your solution. These people can become good sources of information about your competitive position, hidden agendas, or competitive tactics.

Without good inside informants, you are flying through mountains in a fog. If no one is helping you or telling you that you're winning, ask yourself what your real chances are in this deal. Again, if you're not getting signals that you're winning, you're probably not. Good salespeople listen for what their prospects *don't say.*

The Pronoun Shift

One way to tell if you are winning is that as preference grows, people start changing their pronouns and questions from *if* they buy to *when* they buy and from *whom* to *how*. If you've given your presentation and your prospects aren't asking questions about implemen-

If you're not getting signals that you're winning, you're probably not.

tation, risk management, contract issues and support, then you are in trouble. If they are not talking about *how* to do business with you, they are probably not planning to do business with you. This is when you are in that dreadful zone of, "You're not winning, and they aren't telling you."

This is always when salespeople get a terrible amount of misinformation. Not because buyers are mean—although in some cases they are—but they may tell you what they think is true and might not know for sure. Or they might like you personally but not prefer your company or product. Or they may want to keep you in the game as a safety net in case they can't reach terms with the other vendor.

By the time you get to the presentation or proposal, you need more than inside informants—you need power sponsors at high levels. As prospects reach the decision-making phase, politics erupt, and the process can change dramatically. As they approach the crucible of decision, multimillion dollar deals can change in as little as 24 hours. At this point, you need people who really want you to win—people who will give you the information you need, introduce you to the people you need to meet, and go to bat for you with procurement and the decision committee.

Account Management—From Preference to Trust

Many companies define account management objectives in different ways. Some want caretakers, whereas others want to dominate the account by making it so that the customer never has a reason to call a competitor.

To build company-to-company trust, you have to make the first people who choose you look good for doing so. If you

Quality is defined by customer expectations. The salesperson's job is to properly set those expectations high enough to get the business but not so high that you can't deliver.

All awnings leak. Yours do, and so will the next guy's.

One salesperson tells the client, "Our awnings never leak."

Another salesperson instead offers the customer a piece of chalk and tells her, "When the first leak occurs, take this chalk and circle the leak. Call us, and we'll fix it."

Both salespeople may get the sale. But which salesperson will end up with an unhappy customer?

If your competition then says that their awnings don't leak, they may win the initial business, but they won't win the next time. And when that first leak occurs, they will have lost the customer's trust forever.

They may win once, but they will fail to make winning a habit. And that unhappy client is now a vocal negative reference.

overpromise or underdeliver, you make repeat business—where true opportunity lies—an uphill battle. And you end up with a customer base of largely unhappy people.

The purpose of account management is to build company-to-company trust. The gateway is performance and quality *on the first sale.* If you don't exceed expectations on the first sale, you may have inoculated the client against future business.

You have to do more than deliver and perform on the first business—you also have to document your value. The customer will not always do this. If you want to build from rapport to preference to trust, you have to go in and document and publicize what you've done for the client and why it was a good decision to choose you or *keep* you. Rarely will the client go to much effort to dispute these claims if they are reasonable, but it gives ammunition to your supporters.

If you have built trust with powerful individuals in an organization, you then can borrow that trust for access to other people you need to meet. This is called *sponsorship,* and it allows you to radiate successfully to the rest of the organization or industry. The last step of an implementation process is to *proactively* ask your sponsor who else you can be doing this for in the company, in the industry, and in the network. Then you need to ask those people to help you gain access to the people you need to meet.

Equal-Rank Meetings

There are many other things you can do to build company-to-company trust. If top executives can meet each other, this reduces risk because they know that if the salesperson leaves, they still have someone at the top they can call on who has skin in the game. Corporate visits and executive meetings are also important because they assure buyers that there is a company vision that supports the buyer's agenda—that the seller is going to continue to commit resources to product, industry, or geography.

Before Enron became the poster child for corporate abuse (before Ken Lay), the company was one of the best-run organizations in the southwestern United States.

During a very competitive evaluation, Joe Terry had developed relationships with the divisional presidents but had not been able to penetrate to the corporate executives.

Our chairman, John Imlay, was an icon in the industry and known as a very charismatic speaker. He was going to be in Houston to meet a very prestigious client, and Joe took advantage of the trip to arrange a breakfast meeting with the divisional presidents so that he could use John's name to get an audience with the corporate executives.

John made a huge impression on Enron's president and CEO. The CEO asked John, "We are considering investing a substantial amount with your company. What are you going to do to ensure our success?"

John smiled and answered, "I'm going to let Joe make the good decisions he always makes, and everything will work out fine." Baton passed. Deal won. Happy client.

These equal-rank meetings are especially important overseas, where there are greater class differences between managers and non-managers. The executive may say nothing different from what the salesperson has said all along; it's simply that the executive has the stripes. It's important in these executive-to-executive meetings to make sure that trust is left with the account executive after the call.

If the executive steals power during the sales call, he or she can't give it back. That executive is now the actual account manager, and the salesperson is now the gun bearer. Every effort must be made to pass power to the account manager during the sales call. This also reduces vendor abuse if the people inside the account know that you have inside access to executive management.

Relationships

One of the reasons I may trust you and your company is because you solve my problems. The other pillar of trust is personal relationships—moving from alignment to rapport to trust. If I am going to trust you, I have to know that I can depend on you for at least a win-win in every transaction. (Dependability alone is not enough. There are some people I can depend on to stick it to me every time.)

My father-in-law was trusted for 39 years in the insurance business because his clients all knew that he would never do anything to his gain and their detriment. Most of these rural people never quite understood the implications of the insurance they were buying, but they knew he would never do anything that wasn't in their best interest.

This is called *trusted-advisor selling* (the seventh generation of selling), and the height of it is when the buyer says, "I'm not sure what I need. Why don't you study it and tell me what I need. Whatever you're selling, I'm buying." It takes years to build this kind of trust with buyers and only one abuse to break it, but it is the highest level of selling.

Sometimes we trust people only because we know that the risk of loss of future business will keep them honest. Danger comes from sellers who only want to sell to you one time. This is why a contract is still important. Without it, there is really nothing to ensure that trust.

In order to trust you, I need to know that you are dependable. I need to understand your principles and values and trust that you will never do anything that is not in my best interest. Principle-driven people are consistent, not situational. And principles are values acted on consistently.

If that trust grows into personal friendship, this is even better. This is when I not only trust you, but I also enjoy your company. I appreciate your counsel, and you are fun to be around. This is a great benefit to the buyer-seller relationship, but if it doesn't have the underpinnings of strong product or performance, it can melt down quickly.

Even your best sponsors cannot go into implementation saying, "Buy from this guy. I like him. He's my friend." You have to build on both pillars of trust. I trust you because you are an industry expert, you know my business, and you can solve my problems. *Or* I will trust you because we work together, you are my friend, I know your family, and you will never let me down.

In the end, the only thing your company really has to sell is trust. It's at the heart of brand management. Just look at all the images in advertising that focus on trust.

Trust Scorecard

Best Practices, Trust	Importance	Execution			
	Degree of Importance (1 = low, 10 = high)	Agree, but we never do this	We sometimes do this	We often do this	We do this consistently
Individual					
Salespeople are trained in fundamental skills for discovery, linkage, and presentation.					
Opportunity					
We consistently conduct needs assessments with the client before showing our product and solutions.					
We consistently debrief each reference to get perspective of where we are in the sale.					
Account Management					
Our references are developed, rewarded, and their time treated respectfully.					

Best Practices, Trust	Importance	Execution			
	Degree of Importance (1 = low, 10 = high)	Agree, but we never do this	We sometimes do this	We often do this	We do this consistently
We consistently document our value to our existing clients.					
We have earned preferred vendor status in accounts.					
We get exclusive evaluations and noncompetitive business.					
We maintain continuity of the same reps on the same accounts from year to year.					
We conduct customer satisfaction and loyalty assessments regularly.					
Industry/Market					
Our sales force is organized and focused by industry so we can focus on industry-specific solutions for our clients.					

SECTION VII

TRANSFORMATION

TRANSFORMATION— MAKING IT STICK

Until new behaviors are rooted in social norms and shared values, they are subject to degradation as soon as the pressure for change is removed.

John Kotter, "What Leaders Really Do,"
Harvard Business Review, 1999

The best way to predict the future is to create it.

Peter Drucker

Over the past 30 years I've had a lot of managers come to me looking for improvement. Some of them are ready to make drastic changes and are willing to do whatever it takes to solve their business problems. Others aren't comfortable with that much change. They want improvement but not transformation. Others just want a speech. Some want a miracle.

To achieve true competitive advantage, obviously there has to be a lasting top-management commitment to full integration of all sales processes from hiring to training to compensation to team roles and responsibilities, rewards, and performance. To really make it stick, managers have to get back into both deal coaching and performance coaching.

I would start by requiring every manager to read Larry Bossidy and Ram Charan's excellent book, *Execution, the Discipline of Getting Things Done*. It focuses on what it takes to build a culture of execution in all areas. One of my favorite quotes from the book is, "Coaching is the single most important part of expanding others capabilities. It's the difference between giving orders and teaching people how to get things done. Good leaders regard every encounter as an opportunity to coach."

The key is integrating these new processes, embedding them in every aspect of your culture from management language to forecasting, the sales cycle, and compensation.

HOW SALESPEOPLE LEARN: C.A.S.H. LEARNING MODEL

Before you can transform your sales force, you have to understand how adults learn. In addition, salespeople learn differently from other adults. In our experience, there are four steps: *curiosity, awareness, skill,* and *habit* (see Figure 9–1).

Curiosity
Curiosity is the seed of learning—the *individual* has to bring this to the table. In our sessions, we always have a

FIGURE 9–1 C.A.S.H. sales effectiveness change management model.

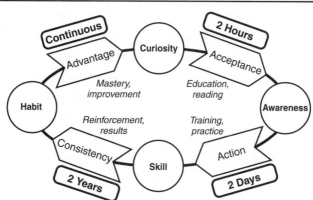

mixture of sponges, vacationers, and prisoners. The first two hours are spent getting the prisoners to unfold their arms. They are prisoners of their own experience.

We have to create a gap between where they are and where they need to be to survive and thrive as the demands of selling and the buyer evolve. They need to understand that they must either grow or go.

Awareness

New awareness is important to personal growth. Reading and training are essential. *By definition, a system cannot change itself from within. It takes outside forces.* But you can't get competitive advantage from awareness alone. It comes from speed of reaction and execution.

For many people, personal growth and development after college often stagnate or are limited to gaining the skills and knowledge needed to perform their current job. For salespeople, however, the competencies required to perform in today's market have escalated because they now need to sell to all levels of their client organizations.

Whether a salesperson is a vice president or not, they need to be conversant with and knowledgeable about C-level issues. However, many salespeople have not developed the necessary strategic literacy in their industries.

Skill

I play golf often and have some skills. I've read almost every book on golf, so I have awareness. I birdie some, par some, and have eagled a few. But Tiger Woods does consistently what I do occasionally (I know, he does some things I'll never do) because he has the discipline to practice incessantly—with his coach—to develop his superior natural physical talents (which I will never have) to their fullest potential. Without this discipline, though, he might be just another trunk slammer, fighting to stay on the tour.

This is also the difference between best-in-class sales organizations and the rest of the pack. The leading sales forces do *consistently* what others do *only some of the time.* In the complex sale, the stakes are huge, and the difference between the winner and the loser is often a very close margin.

Habit

Competitive advantage comes with making skills a *habit*—a permanent, consistent behavioral change at the individual and organizational levels. From awareness to habit is really a two-year process of guided practice.

During the first year, you're telling them. During the second year, you're making them realize that this isn't just the "theme of the month" and that it's here to stay.

Sometimes salespeople decide to just wait a year until the sales manager either gets fired, taking his new processes with him, or fails to follow up. It will take two years of consistent pressure on your part before all your salespeople are finally convinced that the new process is here to stay.

They will begin to get on board when they see others winning using the process. They will make it a personal habit when the company makes it an organizational habit. Every time you don't insist on an activity, strategy session, sales plan, principle, or standard, the cloth of discipline begins to tear.

MAKING IT STICK

Greatness can be nothing unless it's lasting.

Napoléon Bonaparte

An equal challenge is how to make such a process or technology stick with salespeople, who have short attention spans and would rather talk than write. Sales forces have stared down implementations and used passive resistance to outlast scores of multi-million dollar CRM and training initiatives.

Formula for Failure—What Won't Work

- Declare that, "We have a sales problem."

- Implement CRM as a fix.

- Hire a big consulting firm to define your sales cycle (be sure to spend seven figures and take a year). Display the results in a large binder.

- Buy what looks or feels good or what came with your new CRM system.

- Pay less than competitive rates to recruiters.

- Make the form or CRM input very comprehensive (i.e., long), and ask everyone for input.

- Run your training at your sales meeting; make sure that it's the first time your managers have seen it.

- Train your own trainers to save money.

- Hope for adoption, make threats, use guilt, and cheer-lead for results.

- Use revenue as the only metric.

- Excuse veterans from compliance.

Management Commitment: They're Watching You to See If You Are Still Watching Them

This is obvious, of course, but what does it mean? Beyond the customary announcements of top management, it means consistency of execution. Busy salespeople will wait to see if this is just another "theme of the month."

It may seem unnecessary to emphasize that managers must actually attend and help to lead training sessions, but we have seen organizations where this expectation clearly was not set. Every salesperson is watching his or her manager during any rollout for body language, faint praise, passive resistance, or cynicism.

Every failure by management to reinforce the process will cause the fabric of discipline to begin to tear and competitive advantage to slip away. I once passed one of my managers in the hall and asked him about an action item we had agreed on months earlier. He said, "You don't forget about these things, do you?" It was one of the best management compliments I ever received.

Fortunately, the new Web-based tools allow managers to see who is actually using the process on a daily basis. The Fort Hill Company, founded by Cal Wick, has built software so that managers can track action item completion and training follow-through by individual, complete with dashboard and graphics.

"You need to check-up periodically and *let them know that you are looking*. A quick e-mail or some online feedback will put them on notice that you are checking and that you expect execution," Wick says.

According to Wick:

Up until now, most training programs concentrated exclusively on what happened in the classroom. What happened afterwards was a "black hole." In fact, what usually happened was something like this: Sales training put on a course to teach new skills and approaches to optimizing the sales process. In the concluding session, attendees were asked to write a goal for applying what they had just learned. They did. Then they put it in their notebooks, put the notebook on the shelf, and went back to doing what they had done before.

Technology is changing that.

As with the other technologies we discuss, a follow-through system alone is not a solution. To maximize the value of follow-through management technologies,

managers and training professionals need to pay atten-
tion to what is going on. They need to use the system to
track behavior and provide encouragement, recognition,
or correction as necessary.

When that is done, postcourse follow-through tech-
nology increases the impact of sales training and the
value companies realize as a result.

Moreover, adoption needs to be incorporated into comp
plans and performance reviews of all managers for it to really stick.

One of Cal's clients, AstraZeneca wanted to increase
the amount of coaching its sales managers did, so it
ran a program called "Breakthrough Coaching" but
did nothing to ensure that managers followed up on
what they had learned. Not surprisingly, not much
changed in the field.

So the company went back to the drawing board
and developed "Breakthrough Coaching II." The big
difference this time was that the company put a
rigorous system of follow-through in place to make
sure that what was taught was used.

Every manager who attended the program was
required (1) to set two goals for improving their
coaching and (2) to report on progress five times
over a 10-week period. Area and regional managers
had access to the follow-through technology so that
they could see who was doing what they were asked
and who was getting results.

The change was dramatic. Salespeople were polled three months after their managers had attended the program.

- **48** percent reported increased frequency of coaching interactions with their managers.

- **59** percent experienced a shift to a more coaching style of interaction.

- **61** percent felt that their managers were more effective or much more effective as a result.

One summed it up this way: "I am now receiving coaching even when the situation is positive. I used to feel like I only received coaching when I needed to improve on something. I feel like my manager is more in touch with what I am doing."

If you want something to stick, you have to make sure that it is reinforced. The real work begins when the course ends.

It Takes One to Two Years—Do You Have That Long?

Our first step as managers is to expand our time focus. For an *individual,* research shows that it takes about 21 days to form a habit. For an *organization,* it takes *one to two years* of consistent and persistent reinforcement to create organizational habits.

You can get awareness in two hours through a book or a speech. You can start to build skills in a two-day training program. But it may take two years for your salespeople to figure out that you're going to stay with this and for them to actually see the results when they use it versus when they don't.

Real World and Relevant

A successful class alone will not ensure adoption. But a bad one will ensure failure. Word of mouth on the first class will make or break the effort.

The first step toward making a new process stick is to make the training *relevant*. Canned programs won't work anymore. The best training actually involves working *live deals* in class. Similarly, in technology rollouts, salespeople have to see how it helps them with their everyday jobs.

If you use a case study, salespeople will never see their flaws. However, if you have them working their own deals, they see their own flaws—no one has to point them out. This self-discovery of pain creates the curiosity required to start developing new habits.

In our workshops, the first thing we do is add up the dollar volume of all the opportunities/accounts we'll work in class. Then we discuss *how* we're going to create better strategies and action items to make that either a bigger number or increase the probability of reaching that goal.

The transformation is startling. All of a sudden, it's no longer a training class. It's actually working on live deals— *their* competitors, *their* products, *their* issues, and *their* pipeline—and giving them something they can use at 8:30 tomorrow morning. When we focus on deals that are relevant to them, we have very few prisoners in class.

Tailored to Your Unique Sales Process

Before training begins, it is important to define your unique sales cycle and potential action items—built and designed by your people and owned by your managers. This not only makes the process of technology relevant, but it also gains the buy-in of front-line managers, who are the key to adoption.

The worst thing you can have is a sales manager, with arms folded, passing judgment on a new program while you're training the troops. How can such a manager object to a process he or she designed?

Usually front-line sales managers, especially the intuitive ones who are not process-oriented, are hungry for a process to make their people more independent and to give them a coaching tool to keep deals in control. Tying the methodology and their sales process together by phase relates to what they do every day. Real deals mean that the results can be seen immediately. The question that must be answered by the reps is, "Was it worth my time?"

Keep the Tools Simple

The next step is to make any account management or opportunity management planning tool extremely concise. Processes that require salespeople to fill out a 12-page form are destined to fail.

If the integrity of the logical work flow of the tool is not preserved, or if there is excess redundancy, when the tool is integrated with your CRM, you can almost guarantee a failed CRM and a failed methodology.

In a pivotal meeting for us a few years ago, for which I will always be grateful, Phil Wilmington, then senior vice president of worldwide sales for PeopleSoft, said, "We need a one-page sales tool."

I said, "Well, you have the author and owner here. Which of the six P's would you take out?"

He looked at it and said, "None of them. I've got to have them all in order to win."

"Well then, we don't have a methodology issue. What we have is a management issue," I said.

The challenge was discipline. But we did take the razor to our process and drove it down to one page of output and three simple input screens.

It has to be simple, but it also has to be effective. A blank piece of paper is simple, but it's not powerful enough to help you lead a team. And a 12-page document certainly would be complete, but no salesperson is going to slow down enough to use it.

Successful, Credible Instructors—No "Facilitators" Allowed

The next step is to have credible instructors. People who stand up in front of experienced salespeople have to have walked in their shoes, or they will not earn the respect of those people. Lightweight "facilitators" without experience or worn-out salespeople whose experience is not current will not be credible.

In today's marketplace, any instructor has to be involved in sales and have the executive presence to be able to customize the process to the client. Unbelievably, there are legions of sales trainers out there who have never carried a bag or covered a territory. There are ex-product reps out there trying to teach competitive hunting, and there are hunters trying to teach account management. There are ex-reps out there training who have never coached a deal.

Obstacles to Adoption

The character and discipline of an organization are defined by the excuses it allows. And people have no shortage of reasons why change is not needed or why they don't have time for it.

Top 10 Most Common Adoption Subversion Excuses

1. We've had a new sales manager every two years—I can wait this one out.

2. I'm too busy to coach deals.

3. I'm ahead of quota. They won't fire me.

4. I'm a veteran. That stuff is for rookies.

5. I handle the big account. They won't fire me.

6. If I take time to do that and don't make my numbers, they'll fire me anyway.

7. Let's see if my manager has the guts to insist on doing this.

8. I have too much administrative work and no time to coach.

9. Why do we need strategy sessions? We talk to the reps all the time.

10. We've tried this before. This too shall pass.

ON TO THE FOURTH GENERATION: PERPETUAL ADVANTAGE

New Metrics—New Accountability

So what does the future hold? One of the best practices to making processes stick is creating new sales metrics— other than just revenue. Focusing on revenue only as a measurement is like driving in the rear-view mirror.

What is needed are metrics that measure accounts, deals, and salespeople along the way and spot out-of-control performance while there is still time to make changes. Metrics have not been an area of focus, outside of training departments, for the last few years. Salespeople respond well to being measured against goals. *And metrics drive visibility and accountability, which ultimately drives discipline.*

A great book for illustrating the potential effects of new metrics to achieve greater productivity is *Moneyball,* by Michael Lewis.

He writes about how Billy Beane and the Oakland A's baseball organization brought new thinking into how to evaluate which factors predict success for a player. This enabled the team to get high performers for less money and build a perennial winning team without the superhigh payrolls that don't always ensure success.

The "gut-feel" metaphors and stereotypes used by the major league scouts were replaced by new criteria. Beane and his Harvard economists had analyzed what really predicted success in baseball performance—walks taken, on-base percentage, and slugging percentage. They challenged established statistics such as errors—how can you have a statistic based on something you were supposed to do? They saw that the best way to avoid an "error" is to not try, or to be in the wrong place, or to have poor range.

The effect on the scouts and the rest of the league is a classic story of resistance to change management and the difficulties of challenging the intuitive, gut-feel, but untested factors that baseball scouts have used for years.

The power of new metrics changed baseball thinking and performance forever.

As we discussed in the section on technology, a critical best practice is to tie the methodology and customized best practice sales cycle back into the forecast.

New metrics are needed during the coaching phase. There are questions that coaches need to ask salespeople that will challenge assumptions, find blind spots, identify competitive counterstrategies, and drive toward a more successful sales plan.

We have recently implemented with some of our clients a coaching feedback system called Sales Prophet—an analysis of the analysis—that gives a manager's confidence rating of the major questions in the sales plan as a result of the strategy session. The sales executive can then see how and why the forecast has been adjusted by front-line management. This results in fewer surprises and greater confidence in the forecast, as well as a greater win ratio.

235

As a result, there is also a watershed shift in account-ability. Rather than seeing who has filled out forms, the question becomes which managers have strategized and coached their deals? And if not, why not?

Coaching and Forecast Follow-up Metrics

The Internet has created the possibility of getting greater feedback on the pipeline at a minimum of expense and time from the field reps.

While a good coaching session is the foundation of fore-cast accuracy, a manager needs to separate coaching and forecasting techniques. Coaching must be value-added. It needs to provide new ideas to help **Metrics drive visibility and** qualify, advance the strategy, gain **accountability, which** access, challenge assumptions, or **ultimately drive discipline.** brainstorm new ideas. Coaching should expose blind spots for the rep's benefit—not expose his or her shortcomings. These sessions could take an hour or some could take a day depending on the size, importance, and complexity of the deal.

Forecasting reviews should be quick and very focused. They should be driven from the key question areas just dis-cussed: Why will you win? When will it close? What is the source of urgency? What has to happen between now and when it closes? Forecast reviews should take no more than 30 minutes per opportunity. If nothing has changed, five minutes.

A manager should be able to take truthful answers and create a consolidated forecast to pass along. Based on the estimated close date of the opportunity, we have helped a number of our clients *track* the effectiveness of the coaching session and the progress of the deal. First, we can find out if the deal closed at all, if it closed faster than expected, if it closed for more or less than the expected amount, or if we qualified out.

We can ask if the new sales process or technology was helpful or not and, if so, how. We also can determine whether a strategy review was conducted by the sales manager and if it was helpful or not. (This involves more accountability and visibility for the front-line sales managers.) This is also an opportunity for the reps to say where they need help and more follow-up training.

Deal-Tracking Survey

One of the new metrics introduced at Apple to help determine the effectiveness of its training initiative was an Internet survey of over 400 deals that had been coached in strategy review sessions. The beauty of the survey was its efficiency. The survey consisted of a half-dozen questions that branched further only under certain conditions. It didn't take much time to complete.

Rather than just ask why they won or why they lost, it prompted the sales reps about how well they understood the elements of their sales process in the deal. For example, how well did they understand the decision-making process? Did they understand the client's strategic issues? Did they detect a pain that was a source of urgency?

It also asked if the reps had conducted a strategy session with their managers, and if so, was it helpful?

With this metric, managers were able to see that their win ratio when they used the process was significantly higher than when they didn't. They also identified specific areas where salespeople needed more training, which could be done by e-learning modules or reviews.

A very useful outcome was that managers learned that their people weren't qualifying out of enough bad deals. They rewrote their qualification criteria to focus on their more winnable deals.

The last outcome was to identify which managers were conducting strategy sessions and which were not. Interesting phone calls followed. Greater visibility had pushed accountability to the front-line sales managers, where it belonged.

Performance Reviews—More Than Just Deal Competence

> *One of the biggest mistakes companies make is reserving employee performance feedback for the typical annual review.*
>
> Eric Gist and Patrick Mosher, Accenture,
> *The Sales Performance Challenge*

I am still amazed at how many companies don't consistently use performance reviews at all and how many sales organizations use the standard one provided by HR as a way to review salespeople. Based on the effectiveness of most canned reviews, one can understand why.

The best practice is to write performance reviews for salespeople that include the skills, knowledge, and behaviors required to execute your best practices sales cycle. Otherwise, reviews usually are a waste of time.

But there is more to overall performance than deal competency and personality. In addition to competence and chemistry, many salespeople fail because of a lack of commitment, lack of character, lack of communication skills, or lack of cognitive ability to think quickly on their feet.

Deal competency alone may be less than half of overall sales competency, and this can only be measured by observation by sales managers and documented in a performance review designed specifically to measure performance in the field. Figure 9–2 presents a useful diagnostic tool for identifying performance problems in both deal management and the other important elements of overall performance.

Written tests and training session "smile sheets" only measure awareness and acceptance. Assessments on behavioral traits and other things just measure potential. Win-loss reports and numbers just measure deal competency. Only a manager can tell whether the salesperson is competent, as well as committed.

FIGURE 9–2   Sales performance problem diagnostics.

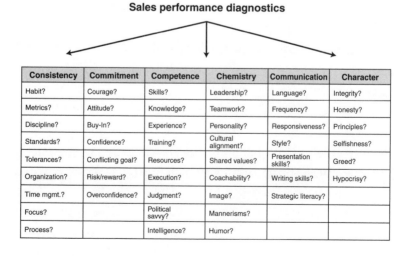

Sales performance diagnostics

Consistency	Commitment	Competence	Chemistry	Communication	Character
Habit?	Courage?	Skills?	Leadership?	Language?	Integrity?
Metrics?	Attitude?	Knowledge?	Teamwork?	Frequency?	Honesty?
Discipline?	Buy-In?	Experience?	Personality?	Responsiveness?	Principles?
Standards?	Confidence?	Training?	Cultural alignment?	Style?	Selfishness?
Tolerances?	Conflicting goal?	Resources?	Shared values?	Presentation skills?	Greed?
Organization?	Risk/reward?	Execution?	Coachability?	Writing skills?	Hypocrisy?
Time mgmt.?	Overconfidence?	Judgment?	Image?	Strategic literacy?	
Focus?		Political savvy?	Mannerisms?		
Process?		Intelligence?	Humor?		

Salespeople become unmotivated because their goals are out of reach, they have lost belief in the company, they have lost belief in the products, or maybe they have personal distractions or have lost confidence all together.

We find that a large number of salespeople fail because of a lack of character. They are not trustworthy. They think selling is a manipulative game. They are not honest with their clients, they are not honest with their managers, and they are not honest with themselves.

Some of them have other businesses on the side. Some of them are not honest with their managers about where they stand in their deals. Some of them set expectations too high, hoping they'll be gone by the time the price has to be paid.

In order to build trust with a client, a person first has to *be* trustworthy. It's not a matter of what they do; it's a matter of who they are. This goes back to the hiring profile and can only be identified after the hire by performance. Obviously, a 360-degree assessment is even better because teammates and customers sometimes will spot this before the sales manager will.

Numbers alone are not always adequate. A sales rep can make his or her number and still lose a lot of business based on the territory's potential. I've seen hot markets where a chimpanzee in a three-piece suit could make quota.

Conversely, I've observed one of the best salespeople I know do everything right and still struggle for a year. A good performance review spotted the problem (we had changed his territory twice—he had been setting up deals that other salespeople closed). Performance observation saved a future star who went on to become an extremely successful performer and manager.

WHAT ABOUT MOTIVATION?

To me, there are two sources of motivation—inside-out and outside-in. One lasts; the other doesn't. I think real motivation comes from inside:

- *A quality solution or product that they feel really helps a customer*—one that the customer will thank them later for selling to them.

- *A solution that can win.* It doesn't have to be superior; it just has to have relative strengths that they can focus on the right prospect without stretching the truth. It must be one in which they can have contagious conviction. Salespeople have to have a playable hand. They can only make up so much gap.

- *Good compensation*—competitive, no-caps, fair, high-upside. In most companies with successful sales forces, a salesperson is often the most highly paid person in direct compensation. And management thinks that this is wonderful because the stock would be sky high if the company had 20 more of them. And *never, never* cut it in the middle of a year unless somehow you think 100 percent sales force turnover is a strategy. (It's happened.)

- *Trips.* It's not just the trip; they can afford the trip. It's the peer and management recognition. And it's being able to go to your spouse and tell them you won them a trip to a very nice place. Visions of warm climates seem to drive salespeople though the snows of December.

- *Personal standards and drivers.* Ambition, ego, self-image, fear of poverty, achievement mentality—I've seen them all work.

- *Working for good management that they can trust and the opportunity for personal growth.*

- *Achievable goals.* Make 'em stretch—but an unattainable goal will demotivate a sales force faster than anything.

- *A support organization that will help the sales force create a great buying experience for the customer and make them feel good about what they sold.*

If you *don't* have these things, a motivational speech, cheerleading, or a merchandise contest won't help. If you *do* have these things, you don't need the others. Focus your speakers on achieving the preceding.

Primary Intelligence has an excellent "Sales Confidence Index" survey that actually measures confidence of sales forces in the preceding factors. If your salespeople don't believe in your company and your solutions, then they can't sell them with conviction, and you may not know until too late without third-party feedback.

Win-Loss Reviews—The Silver Bullets of Truth
Another great metric is a win-loss analysis by a third-party organization. The words of the client as to why you won or lost are the silver bullets of truth.

Companies such as Primary Intelligence create win-loss reports that are invaluable and *must be conducted by an outside third party*. These reports collect information and feedback as to why you lost so that you don't make the same mistake over and over again. This information is pure gold (and you are going to pay for it in one way or another) and needs to be refreshed on an almost-daily basis.

It will help salespeople learn from win-loss reports if they first accept that *all losses are the result of being outsold*. Some will say that they were just in the wrong deal. If this is the case, and they stayed until the end, they were outsold.

In the case of the "lesser product" excuse, if they *sometimes* win with the lesser product due to superior selling, then they must have been outsold. If price is the excuse for the loss, why didn't they find that out earlier?

It has been said that there are three things that can happen in a deal: You can win, walk, or get outsold. In reality, there are four. You can also lose to no decision after wasting resources.

You can create your own win-loss reports, but the answers are almost always predictable. "We won because of superior salesmanship" or "We lost because of price and product." You might as well have them preprinted.

The only caution or filter required to make the best use of this information is to remember that customers are making an emotional and political decision in the end. However, when they give answers about their decisions, they will say that the decisions were logical and rational.

The key is knowing how to dig down into the political and emotional dynamics of the deal. An effective third-party company calling on the customer will uncover incredible things about preparation, personality, politics, competitive strategies, failure to link into issues, and misreading of accounts. They are a treasure trove of corrective information.

PERPETUAL ADVANTAGE COMPETITIVE CYCLE SPEED—GET AHEAD AND STAY AHEAD

> *Sustaining advantage requires continuous improvement and change, not a static solution in which strategy can be set and forgotten.*
>
> Michael Porter

> *Speed has become an important element of strategy.*
>
> Regis McKenna

Execution, rather than awareness, is at the heart of making winning a habit. Speed and consistency of execution and innovation are the path to *sustainable* competitive advantage (see Figure 9–3).

Feedback from all these sources and metrics should cause sales forces to continuously evaluate personnel, sales messages, product offerings, value propositions, and customer loyalty. If these are well implemented and used effectively, the result is a move from inconsistent, up and down results to perpetual advantage.

We discussed in an earlier chapter how Col. John Boyd revolutionized military thinking and maneuver warfare. His acronym for competitive cycle speed in a fighter plane

FIGURE 9–3 Competitive cycle perpetual advantage process and metrics.

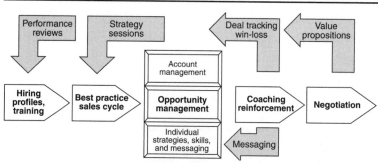

and then a military unit was the OODA loop. OODA stands for *o*bserve, *o*rient, *d*ecide, and *a*ct, and it changed everything.

Winning pilots or winning generals get information *faster* than the opponent, process it faster, and react more quickly according to principles to gain an advantage in every situation. It isn't the plan but the *speed and effectiveness of the adjustment process* that gives them the advantage.

Speed and accuracy of information drive speed and accuracy of strategy, which drive competitive advantage. The battles of Napoléon, Nelson, Jackson, and Patton, as well as many marketing campaigns, all teach us this lesson from history.

New technologies can enable the right metrics and adjustment processes without requiring additional input from sales reps to slow them down.

If you can measure in less than one year which salespeople can drive a complex sale, if you can detect and correct deals that are out of control at each phase of the cycle, if you can improve messages in response to the competition within 48 hours, if you can improve your sales cycle model and hiring profile with every win or loss—then you and your sales organization can get ahead, stay ahead, and achieve *perpetual advantage*. Somebody's going to do it right first. Will it be you?

SUMMARY: TRAIL MAP TO TRANSFORMATION

1. Establish realistic expectations with upper management.

2. Assess your individual and organizational pains.

3. Compare these pains with your vision—identify your performance gaps.

4. Prioritize your initiatives:

   • Build a management team that shares your vision.

   • Upgrade quickly those who can't or won't improve.

   • Define your own best sales cycle model.

   • Build a new hiring profile for reps; repeat upgrade.

   • Re-examine your messaging positioning.

   • Train on the methodology using your unique sales cycle and live accounts.

   • Only then automate your process, giving reps what they need to win.

- Build your methodology into your forecast, performance reviews, compensation, and hiring profile.

5. Execute change while selling; you can't stop to rebuild.

6. Document some quick wins to build belief and trust.

7. Reinforce coaching discipline to make winning a habit.

8. Introduce new metrics for accountability, continuous improvement, and perpetual advantage without slowing the reps down.

Transformation Scorecard

Best Practices, Transformation	Importance	Execution			
	Degree of Importance (1 = low, 10 = high)	Agree, but we never do this	We sometimes do this	We often do this	We do this consistently
Individual					
We conduct sales-specific performance reviews for salespeople that include the specific skills, knowledge, and behaviors required to execute our best practices sales cycle.					
Opportunity Management					
Training is relevant and involves working live deals in class.					
We have a coaching feedback system from strategy sessions that is a part of our forecast.					
We have a presentation and messaging feedback system to measure presentation effectiveness.					

Best Practices, Transformation	Importance	Execution			
	Degree of Importance (1 = low, 10 = high)	Agree, but we never do this	We sometimes do this	We often do this	We do this consistently
Account Management					
We have a closed-loop sales and marketing system that integrates sales, service, marketing, and design.					
Managers attend and help lead training sessions.					
Managers can track action item completion and training follow-through by individual.					
Industry/Market					
We have a top-management commitment to full integration of all sales processes—training, compensation, rewards, hiring, and tools.					
Our feedback and innovation processes keep our competition reacting to our initiatives.					

APPENDIX

R.A.D.A.R.®–SIX P'S OF WINNING A COMPLEX SALE

As described in detail in *Hope Is Not A Strategy*, R.A.D.A.R.® is an opportunity management process for controlling competitive evaluations involving politics, strategic solutions, competition, and decision-making processes by committees. This section provides greater detail on the six-P process, so that this book will be complete in itself. If you have already read *Hope,* this is a review.

Link Solutions to Pain

The first step in the process is to understand the client's *pain* (or *gain*). What problem is the client trying to solve? A dormant pain is a problem clients don't even know they have compared with an active pain that they have not only acknowledged but for which they are actively seeking a solution.

Active pains already have money budgeted and teams working with vendors to find a solution. But if you can uncover a dormant problem, elevate it to an active pain,

In fact, how well and quickly you review and revise your plan is more important than the perfection of the original plan.

and effectively link your solution to solving it, you gain competitive advantage.

When linking your solution to a benefit, remember to ask yourself what the customer is *always* thinking: "*So what? What does it mean to me?*" Failing to answer this question leaves the job of linking your solution to the client's business pain up to the client, which results in a loss of control and perceived value of your solution. You need to make sure to sell strategic benefits to strategic buyers and sell technical benefits to tactical buyers.

Qualify the Prospect

How you qualify a *prospect* depends on the number of opportunities in your pipeline and your available resources. The first question you should ask yourself when qualifying a prospect is, "Will this business happen for anyone at all?"

Many deals are lost to "No decision." This is so for two reasons: Either the business pain that you solve is not urgent enough to act upon or there is no political sponsor strong enough to push it through. The pain needs to be strong enough and emotional enough to drive change and create a source of urgency, or else the deal will sit on the forecast.

The next question should be, "Is this a good opportunity for us?" Keep in mind that in many evaluations the client has already decided who they are going to buy from.

Build Competitive Preference

There is a wide range of *preference* in complex sales ranging all the way from disclosure, where the client is telling you what you need to know to help you win, to the highest level, trust, where they're buying whatever you're selling. There is also a spectrum of negative preference, which ranges from skeptical to even open hostility.

In the last 20 years, some methodologies also have taught building preference with *everybody*. We disagree. First of all, there isn't time. Second, it isn't necessary. Third, it can actually be counterproductive. Not that we should ever alienate anyone, but based on the decision-making process and the roles people play, we can win the business by focusing our preference-building efforts on the people who have the most impact on the decision.

Building preference in all directions, without a strategy, is a waste of time. Selling to everyone equally not only spreads your efforts too thin, but it can help the competition. For example, the people down on the hostile end of the scale are probably too far gone. The other problem is that they often don't *act* hostile. They may be very nice to you, when, in fact, they are taking everything you give them and passing it straight to the competition.

The pain needs to be strong enough and emotional enough to drive change and create a source of urgency or else the deal will sit on the forecast.

In account strategy sessions, we see people pounding away on these antagonists in the hope of winning everyone's vote, sending pounds and pounds of literature and wasting sales calls. Based on the decision-making process, if a complete consensus is not required, we may be able to win without their vote. They may not even *have* a vote.

And don't confuse access or politeness with preference. Just because they will meet with you and are nice to you doesn't mean they will sponsor you. The quality of relationships, from the salesperson's view, is the most frequently misread and overestimated part of a salesperson's plan.

You need to know not only *if* people are for you but also *how strongly* they are for you. When the pressure builds, you need to know if they are going to fold their cards.

To build competitive preference in an opportunity, you have to establish the political point of entry and then effectively differentiate your company and solution and build positive mindshare with key influencers—before your competition does it.

At the account level, building preference in the long run means overdelivering on what you sold them. Then you need to move from *loyalty* to *trust* by never giving them a reason to go to anyone else. You have to make your sponsors look good for having chosen you.

Determine the Decision-Making Process
Before you can drive an effective strategy, you have to understand the client's decision-making *process*. This is different from the client's evaluation process. It is also different from the approval process (see Figure A-1).

As most competitive evaluations progress, there is a point where they turn from logical and rational to emotional and political. This is typically because the principals have not reached a consensus and have divided camps. Because they can't find everything they want from a single vendor, they often can't agree on what their priorities are. Sometimes the result is a power struggle, where multimillion dollar deals flip in a matter of hours.

FIGURE A-1   The crucible.

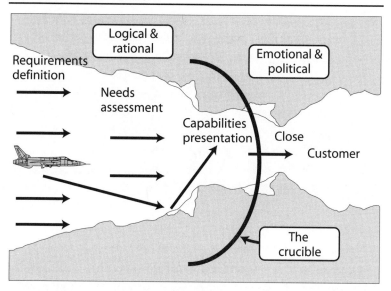

We use the metaphor of the canyon and the crucible to describe this dynamic. The *canyon* is the narrowing list of vendors with only one survivor (it's not a funnel—gravity, nor large numbers do anything for you). The *crucible,* as in chemistry, is where political pressure builds, the decision process melts down, and tempers often explode.

In other cases, clients can find a solution from several vendors, and the issues shift to non-product differentiators. Some evaluations stall out altogether from increased risk, low value, or lack of sponsorship.

As one of our clients said, "They don't decide how to decide until they can't decide." Things move fast in the crucible, which means that strategy revision should be daily and dynamic.

When Jack Barr was selling to Lockheed Martin for SAP Software, the evaluation committee at Lockheed included 207 members. But, in reality, the decision was made by only five people.

Though those five were positioned as only a *part* of a democratic vote, it was really an algebraic democracy. Both Jack and his competitor knew this, but the competitor didn't believe it.

In the end, Jack concentrated his efforts on the right people and won.

Decisions in a buying committee often are reached by what we call *algebraic democracy.* Although most people have some sort of vote, some votes count more than other people's votes. While some votes count x, other votes count $5x$, and some votes equal the sum of all other votes plus one. This is a blind spot in most sales plans. Other decisions may be by department or autocratic or may be two-tiered.

Sell to Power

In an organization, *power* is both invisible and dynamic. Some power comes from positional authority, but many people hold personal power and influence without a powerful title.

To make things even more complicated, people within a company gain and lose power every day. You have to be able to identify power in a prospect account and win the prospect's support early on in the sales cycle. Start early figuring out multiple navigation routes to powerful people. If you can build preference and win the hearts of the powerful people, they will help you win the votes you need.

You also can borrow power from one person to gain access to someone else. In the very beginning, start asking questions about political power so that you can find out who has it and where you should spend your time.

Develop and Communicate the Plan

Some methodologies have defined strategy at *only* the account or opportunity level—frontal (price and product superiority), flanking (changing the pain, process, or power), fractional (divide and conquer or take a slice), and timing (delay or accelerate). These are important models, but without a *plan* for how to win the hearts of *each individual stakeholder* or to *live without their vote*, you have a strategy in name only. You have the *what* but not the *how-to* action items to execute your plan.

A winning strategy enables you to anticipate events and communicate your plan. Complex sales strategies must be driven at the industry, enterprise, opportunity, and individual levels. Without a plan, you are at risk of having more than one salesperson on an account saying the wrong things to the wrong people.

Collaboration is critical to the extended sales team. Not only do you have to have a clear strategy, but you also have to be able to communicate the plan to the team. Everyone on the team must know the goals and objectives and must be accountable for their part.

Additionally, you need to have a plan B. Once you have tested your plan, develop alternative strategies. Bad news early is good news because you can still change your plan. Like poker, the worst outcome is to finish second, late after you've spent your resources.

BIBLIOGRAPHY

Larry Bossidy, Ram Charan, and Charles Burck, *Execution: The Discipline of Getting Things Done.* New York, New York: Crown Business, 2002.

Marcus Buckingham and Donald Clifton, *Now, Discover Your Strengths.* New York, New York: The Free Press, 2001.

Robert Coram, *Boyd: The Fighter Pilot Who Changed the Art of War.* New York, New York: Back Bay Books, 2002.

Neil Rackham and John DeVincentis, *Rethinking the Sales Force: Redefining Selling to Create and Capture Customer Value.* New York: McGraw-Hill, 1999.

Jim Dickie and Barry Trailer, *Sales Effectiveness Insights— 2005 State of the Marketplace Review.* Bolder, CO: CSO Insights, 2005.

Howard Gardner, *Frames of Mind: The Theory of Multiple Intelligences.* New York, New York: Basic Books, 1983.

Bill Hybels, *Courageous Leadership.* Grand Rapids, MI: Zondervan, 2002.

Michael Lewis, *Moneyball: The Art of Winning an Unfair Game.* New York: Norton, 2004.

Jeffrey Pfeffer and Robert I. Sutton, *The Knowing-Doing Gap: How Smart Companies Turn Knowledge into Action.* Cambridge, MA: Harvard University Press, 2000.

Chet Richards, *Certain to War: The Strategy of John Boyd Applied to Business.* Philadelphia, PA: XLibris Corporation, 2004.

THE COMPLEX SALE, INC.

3015 Windward Plaza; Suite 475
Alpharetta, GA 30005
Phone: 770–360–9299
Web: www.complexsale.com

Around the globe, in more than 50 countries, The Complex Sale, Inc., teaches sales teams the processes and skills they need to achieve competitive advantage.

R.A.D.A.R.®—Winning Opportunity Strategies is a proven opportunity management methodology and live-account workshop that enables salespeople to win the competitive, political sales evaluation.

Total Enterprise Account Management® (T.E.A.M.) enables sales forces to build company-to-company relationships in strategic or global accounts.

Best Practices Sales Cycle Workshops for your sales management team to capture the best practice sales cycle unique to your organization, target market, and value proposition.

Coaching the Complex Sale provides managers with a deep understanding of their role as coaches of the sales and business processes implemented by your organization.

FORe—Forecast Opportunity Reviews are one-day workshops designed to install a common language and methodology for coaching opportunity strategies and avoiding forecast surprises.

P.R.I.S.M.® Preemptive Integrated Sales Messaging solves the knowledge-transfer problem between marketing and sales. Build a playbook that the salesperson can use to provide buyers with compelling, differentiated messages.

Bonfire of Management Principles is a three-day tactical management program designed to create a winning performance culture of standards, tolerances, principles, and expectations among your management team.

Negotiating for Value Workshops address specific issues your sales team will face in maintaining value in a negotiation resulting in lower discounts and better margins.

Sales Strategy Execution Series is a series of individual skills-development courses that teach salespeople how to execute selling strategies.

Global Planning for Sales (GPS) suite of software products integrates with your CRM system and enables the methodologies of The Complex Sale in a simple, yet powerful fashion.

INDEX

261

Index